ANIMALS, INC.

ANIMALS, INC.

A BUSINESS PARABLE
for the
21ST CENTURY

KENNETH A. TUCKER
AND VANDANA ALLMAN

WARNER
BUSINESS
BOOKS™

NEW YORK   BOSTON

Copyright © 2004 by The Gallup Organization
All rights reserved.

Warner Business Books
Warner Books

Time Warner Book Group
1271 Avenue of the Americas, New York, NY 10020.
Visit our Web site at www.twbookmark.com.

The Warner Business Books logo is a trademark of Warner Books.

Printed in the United States of America
First Printing: February 2004
10 9 8 7 6 5 4 3 2 1

Library of Congress Cataloging-in-Publication Data

Tucker, K. A.
    Animals, Inc. : a business parable for the 21st century / Kenneth A. Tucker
and Vandana Allman.—1st Warner Books ed.
        p. cm.
    ISBN 0-446-53049-2
    1. Management—Philosophy. 2. Success in business. I. Allman, Vandana. II.
Title.
    HD31.T784 2004
    658.4'09—dc22   2003022079

Book design by Giorgetta Bell McRee

To Judy, my helpmate, and my children, Kendra, Kristen, and Kenny, who are the fuel and spark for my imagination.

—Ken

For my best friend and husband, Jeff, who always creates a clear path for us with his love and support.

—Vandana

ANIMALS, INC.

In memory of Donald O. Clifton,
who taught us all to soar with our strengths.

ONE

Scarecrow looked out protectively over the Goode Farm through his navy blue plastic button eyes. It was a perfect spring morning, and the slight breeze made his straw tingle. It felt good to be sort of alive. At first glance, everything seemed to be in perfect harmony. The cows and horses were brunching in the upper meadow, in the barnyard the pigs were teaching their piglets to play in the mud, over in the henhouse was Clara complaining loudly, as usual, and by the pond the sheep were busy admiring their coiffures in the reflection and rearranging their almost perfect curls, also as usual. In front of the farmhouse the dogs were lying still, waiting for Farmer Goode to . . .

Then he saw it. Or maybe he just felt the slightest change in the breeze. But everything he'd learned during the twelve years he'd spent working in this field made him certain something was wrong. He listened, and thought he heard the whisper of flapping wings. Slowly, deliberately, he scanned the blue, blue sky. A yellow and red butterfly glided gracefully across the horizon. A coterie of bees buzzed past hurriedly on their way to work. And finally, he saw him, Chucky the Crow. Sitting innocently on the telephone wire, actively ignoring Scarecrow as if he wasn't standing right there.

Chucky made a big show of staring somewhere way off into the distance, shading his eyes with a wing, while he nonchalantly whistled a ragged tune. "Me?" his whole attitude seemed to say. "Me steal a couplea bites of your precious seeds? Hey, pal, you got the wrong bird. I just stopped here for a short rest on my way back to the nest. Didn't even realize there was a good square meal around."

Then their eyes met. They glared at each other for a few seconds. If Scarecrow had had lips he would have smiled. He'd won again. Chucky leaped into the breeze and without even a backward glance, he was gone.

Scarecrow watched as Chucky disappeared into the distance. For a moment he relaxed. Once again, he realized with great pride, he'd done his job, he'd protected his field. But this time, for some reason, that odd feeling he had that something was wrong didn't go away. It irritated him, like a ladybug playing hopscotch on his back. Later that night, he would find out how right he was.

Farmer Goode banged the canning jar on the table and called the meeting to order. Every animal on the farm had crammed into the barn, except the horses, Jesse and Queenie, who poked their heads inside through the open window. Lawrence the Owl and a gang of teenaged pigeons who called themselves "The Hawks" sat on the rafters, and several generations of rodents crowded together near the entrance to their holes. Everybody was nervous. Normally Farmer Goode held the annual stock meeting in the winter, after the harvest, to tell everyone how well the farm was doing. For as long ago as anyone could remember, there had never been a barn meeting in the spring.

"I have some news for you," Farmer Goode began. He paused, and a tear formed in his eye. "I'm going to be moving off the place. I'm off to Greener Pastures."

"Neigh," protested Jesse, whose cry was heard above a great wave of protests.

Farmer Goode raised his hand for silence. He had no choice, he explained, he was just too old to work the farm himself and there were no Goode men left. "So I've got no choice. I'm moving into the Greener Pastures Retirement Home."

"But . . . but what will happen to us?" Clara the Chicken clucked nervously. "Some of us . . . some of the other girls are too old to find another job." As she said this she looked directly at Henrietta, who cackled, "Right, like you're some spring chicken," and turned away in disgust.

Scarecrow stood rigidly in a corner. A seed of sweat

appeared on his forehead. He'd always believed his job was secure. He'd made no plans for his future. He had neither a nest nor an egg.

"Now, now, that's why I've called this meeting," Farmer Goode continued. "You all know how much this place means to me . . ." The animals knew the history of the farm. The Goode family had made its home here for many generations, and in fact some of the animals could trace their own families back almost as far. Farmer Goode himself had been born on this land more than eighty years earlier. The Goode family struggled through three droughts and the Great Depression—although Farmer Goode never understood what was so great about it—and there was the cyclone of '52. Through it all the Goode Farm had survived. The animals had always agreed, this was "a Goode place to be."

Several times in the past few years developers had looked enviously at the land, commenting that it would be the perfect spot for a first-rate shopping mall. They made fine offers, but Farmer Goode always turned them down flat.

But now it was time for Farmer Goode to go live where folks could give him the help he needed. "You animals have been like family to me since Ma Goode passed," he said, "so I can't let you down. But you have to decide what you want to do . . ."

There were only two options, he explained. He could sell the land to the mall developers and use the money to find a comfortable place for just about everybody. He knew of some excellent petting zoos and small farms where they could live out their lives peacefully. Or he would allow them to run the farm themselves. "Just hand over the reins, so to speak," he said. "But I have to warn you, that won't be easy. These last few years . . . well, there's been some problems I've kept from you. Maybe some of you noticed that when things got broke around here they didn't get fixed quick as they used to, and that sometimes meals were a little skimpy. I got to be honest with you, if you decide to try to run this place yourselves, you're gonna have some tough days ahead. Farming is a tough business. It's up to you, though."

For a few seconds there was complete silence as the impact of this announcement sank in—and then everybody panicked. Leave the farm! Move! Find a new job! Impossible! Can't do it! Some of the animals started running in circles, desperately chasing their tails. The cows just flopped right down in utter shock. The chickens scampered about wildly as if they'd lost their heads, complaining to anyone who would listen.

Finally Big Mo, who had lived on the farm longer than any other animal, took control. "Stop!" he shouted. "Everybody quiet down. You, chickens, shut your beaks." To his great surprise, they all listened to him. And then they looked to him for instructions.

The big pig waddled slowly to the front of the barn. In human years Mo was the oldest animal on the farm. Everyone respected him for his age, wisdom, and experience. It was widely rumored—although no one remembered where the rumor had begun—that when he was younger he had been offered the leading role in *Babe* but turned it down to stay on the farm. While Mo refused to confirm that story, no one ever heard him deny it either. "All right, animals," he said, turning to face the assembled stock, "we've got a decision to make. Either we spend the rest of our lives making cutesy faces at kids while they pull on our ears or we run this place ourselves. So what's it going to be?"

"Mo," Abe the Goat pointed out, "whattya talking? We don't know nuthin' about running this place."

"Excuse me for butting in, Abe," Beau the Bull said in his deep, sonorous voice. Beau, actually Beauregarde Mounthatten IV, the great-grandson of a world champion and a bull who might have competed himself but for a gnarled forelock, never said very much, but when he did speak he made good sense. "Fact is, these last few years Farmer Goode couldn't have run this place without our help. We're already doing all the work around here—and doing a pretty good job of it too. If we all pull together, we can do it."

One of the duck quintuplets quacked softly, "I don't want to leave here. This is the only pond I know."

Mary the Sheep snapped angrily, looking right at Abe, "Listen you old goat, maybe you like hearing kids tell you how cute you are, but if I hear 'Mawy had a wittle wamb' one more time, I swear I'm gonna go fricassee." Turning to Mo, she said, "Where do I sign?"

The barn erupted with enthusiasm. Never before had all the animals agreed so completely on anything. Even the house dogs and the barn cats raised their tails and slapped each other high-ones. When it quieted down Mo said they needed to vote to make it official. "We'll take a straw poll."

"Oooh," moaned Scarecrow when he heard that. But then he dutifully began handing out his hand and much of his arm, reminding everyone to please return their straw after voting. He knew from experience it would still take him most of the night to get his fingers back in place.

Abe was the only animal to take a straw against the plan. "Listen," he pleaded, "what do we know from running a business? You want to know about chewing cud? That we know. But believe me, you're all gonna lose your hide."

The animals ignored him: They were going to run the farm! Farmer Goode agreed that he would make all the legal arrangements to transfer ownership, telling them, "I guess you could call this the first real stock ownership plan in history."

The meeting ended with Mo asking everyone to give Farmer Goode a big ground of applause for everything he'd done, and every animal thumped hard on the dirt floor.

Mo graciously accepted the position of President and Chief Executive Animal. He moved with his wife, Princess, and their three little piglets into the Goode home, hung up his beloved chalk-on-velvet painting of Noah's Ark, then set to work learning how to run the farm. "The door to my office is always open," he announced. That was definitely true: As animals had difficulty turning a doorknob, Jesse kindly kicked off the door.

It was quite an experiment. Animals had never successfully run a farm before, and just about everyone in the county watched with great interest. But no one watched with more interest than Mr. Edward Biggs, chairman of Biggs Business, the biggest shopping center construction firm in the region.

Biggs was a large man, slightly rounded with age. His face was thick and reddish. Large jowls hung down from his cheeks like pouches, and his gray sideburns were clipped well below his angular ears.

Biggs was the kind of visionary who could look once at a piece of beautiful farmland and know immediately what type of factory would be best suited for that location. It was a talent that had made him a wealthy man. Long ago he had fixed his beady eyes on the Goode Farm. Several times he had made quite reasonable offers to Farmer Goode for his land and had never quite understood the old man's reluctance to sell.

The very day that Farmer Goode packed his bags and moved to Greener Pastures, Biggs set up a meeting with Mo at the farm. Lily the Lamb, the new receptionist, greeted him cordially. "You want a cup of fresh milk while you wait?" she asked. "I can get it direct from the container."

"Oh no, my little lamb," Biggs said sweetly, sweeping off his hat and bowing deeply. "But I must ask you, who does your wool? It's really quite striking."

"Really," Lily said, casually licking a curl into place, "oh, it's sort of . . . natural."

Before Biggs could respond Mo appeared in the doorway and led him into the parlor. Waiting there were Jesse, the big stallion representing the farm's workers, and Lawrence the Owl, representing management. Mo had appointed them to these very important positions because they had been on the farm almost as long as he had, which meant that they had more experience than anybody else.

"It's called seniority," Mo had explained carefully to Jesse, "I read all about it. It's a really important thing to have. But you can't learn it or buy it or even take training courses to get it. Nobody can teach it. You can't earn it, and no matter how good you are at your job, they can't give it to you. When you have it you get the most important jobs. It's simple. See, Jesse, you've been here the longest, except for me, so you must be the most qualified, otherwise you wouldn't have been here so long."

Lawrence too had been impressed to learn he had seniority. In fact, Mo made it sound so good when he explained it that Lawrence secretly wished he could have had it a long time ago. Or at least some of it.

Jesse and Lawrence were seated by the fireplace when Mo and Biggs entered, although Jesse was squirming, trying without success to get comfortable on the large couch.

"How do you do, gentleme . . . animals," Biggs began. "Ed Biggs . . ." Instinctively, he reached out with his hand toward Lawrence for a handshake, but caught himself and saved embarrassment by faking a cough, and raising his hand to cover his mouth. Instead, he nodded politely. "Thank you for agreeing to meet with me. I think you'll find what I have to say of particular interest."

"Can I get you a can of water?" Mo asked, "or a piece of garbage?"

"No, no," said Biggs, "nothing at all, thank you. Frankly, Mr. . . . Mr. . . . Mr. . . ." Biggs's voice wound down like a battery running out of power.

"Look, Biggs," Mo said, "maybe you didn't notice, but the truth is that I'm a pig."

Biggs unsuccessfully tried to feign surprise. Stalling for time, he adjusted his own glasses. "Well, I wouldn't say that you . . ."

"Oh, please. Didn't you notice this snout? You think maybe that's an ordinary nose? Let's be honest, Biggs, have you ever done business with a real pig before?"

"Well," Biggs said, "metaphorically speaking, certainly, but in actuality, I suppose . . ."

"And them," Mo continued, pointing a hoof toward Jesse and Lawrence. "Didn't it seem a little strange to you that there's a horse sitting there on the sofa?"

"Well, obviously I recognized the fact that he is a horse," Biggs responded, "but I want you to know that that doesn't make any difference to me. I don't discriminate against any . . . species. Business is business, I always say. And we're all equal in the eyes of the Internal Revenue Service.

"Look, I'm not here to waste time swatting flies. As you may know, you're sitting on a valuable piece of property. I'm authorized by Biggs Construction to make a very sizable offer for it."

Mo had found an old pair of Ma Goode's spectacles in a desk drawer and fumbled to put them on. Much too small, they balanced precariously on the end of his large snout. While he couldn't see through them, he felt they added an authoritative touch. "I'm sorry, Mr. Biggs, but this land is not for sale."

"Now now, don't be so hasty. Suppose I said I could pay you enough money so that you could be rolling in . . . in . . . mud. Just imagine," he said with a broad sweep of his arm, "mud as far as you can see. All the beautiful brown mud you ever dreamed of. Enough mud for your whole family, all your little piggies."

Mo shook his head. "Look, Mr. Biggs, it doesn't matter how much you offer. We've all agreed; we're not selling this place."

"Neigh," Jesse said firmly.

Biggs clasped his hands in front of him and chuckled. "Well, I have to admit that you drive a very hard bargain. All right, you win. I'm going to be frank with you. This is my very best offer." With that, he began writing a figure on a piece of paper.

"Noooooo," Lawrence the Owl said. "Nooooooo."

Biggs paused. "You don't even know what the number is."

"It doesn't matter," Mo told him. "This land is not for sale."

Biggs put down the pen, looked directly at Mo, and said, "Now don't you think you're being a little bit . . . *pigheaded* about this?"

Lawrence laughed. For those who, like Biggs, have never heard an owl laugh, it sounds like walnuts being pureed in a blender. Biggs was stunned at the sound and stared at Lawrence. "Of course he's pigheaded," Lawrence explained logically, "he's a pig."

Jesse laughed too, a big hearty horse-laugh.

Biggs's face turned bright red. He definitely was not used to being laughed at by an owl and a horse. "Hey," he snapped angrily at Jesse.

"Where?" Jesse asked, looking around the room.

"Now just listen to me," Biggs said to Mo. "I don't know what you expect to do with this land, but I'm warning you . . ."

"It's a farm," Mo said softly, "and we're going to farm it."

"Who?" Biggs asked suspiciously, wondering if one of those megafarmglomerates had beaten him to the deal.

"Whoo," responded Lawrence, instinctively.

"Us," Mo told him, his short, curly tail starting to wiggle involuntarily with excitement. Mo was known to have a particularly stoic tail that rarely revealed his emotions, but the prospect of all the animals and rodents and birds working paw-in-wing to make the farm successful filled him with joy. "All of us," he said proudly. "The biggest and the smallest, the ground-huggers and the sky-sailors. All of us."

Biggs leaned forward until his face was only inches from the end of Mo's snout and snarled, "And what makes you think you know how to run a farm?"

"Well," Mo gulped, "we were doing it when Farmer Goode was here."

Jesse added, "We were already doing . . ."

"Hogwash!" Biggs snapped.

Mo was stunned at the insult.

Biggs blundered on. "You think it's that easy, do you? Let me tell you something. Running a farm is like running a business, and what do you know about running a business? Nothing! You know NOTHING about that!"

Lawrence's wings fluttered from the force of Biggs's anger. But Mo didn't even flinch. "Maybe not yet," he was forced to agree. "But it can't be that hard. We just have to sell our products for more money than it costs to run the farm. That's business."

Biggs slowly shook his head. "It's impossible," he said, "completely impossible. Do you even know what P&L means? Spreadsheets? R&D? Depreciation? Marketing? You know how to meet OSHA regulations? Have you got the proper access to all your buildings required by the Americans with Disabilities Act? Core competencies?"

The words shot out of his mouth as if from a machine gun. The power of his words literally raised him out of his chair until he was standing over Mo shouting at him. "Gross revenues? Liability insurance? Do you have a pay scale? Pension funds? Stock options?

Promotions? Risk management? Withholding? Have you ever tried to hire a bull? Or fire a chicken?" His words thundered through the room, out the windows and beyond, to the barns, the stables, and into the fields where all the animals heard them. "Mark my words, you'll fail. Fail! And when you do, I will be standing there to pick up the pieces. Someday, very soon, a shopping mall will rise right where I'm standing. And I promise you, the first shop to be opened will be . . ." His eyes narrowed and he spat out his threat: ". . . a butcher shop!"

Even Mo shivered at the thought.

"Good day, you . . . animals! We'll meet again, I promise you—preferably at dinner," Biggs said and laughed viciously. He stormed out of the farmhouse. As he disappeared down the lane he was heard repeating over and over, "At dinner!" and laughing maniacally.

No one in the parlor made a sound until the last strains of Biggs's threats floated away on the breeze. Then Jesse brayed softly, "You know, Mo, there are a lot of good things to be said about a nice comfortable pasture."

TWO

At first, Biggs's dreams of the great mall would be foiled. Every morning at sunrise Rocky "Red" Rooster would proudly wake the farm. All of the animals and birds and rodents went dutifully about their chores, just as they had done when Farmer Goode had been in charge. In the new spirit of cooperation, those animals able to perform additional tasks voluntarily did so. And so the cows were milked and the eggs were collected and the fields were tended. Meals were served, although not always on schedule or as filling as they had been, and no one went hungry.

But Biggs had no intention of giving up. He hired the law firm of Power & Money to investigate the legal situation. While only in literary fiction had animals ever been known to operate a farm, the clerks at the law firm could find no legal barriers to prevent it. In response to a letter sent to the Department of Agriculture Biggs was informed that "while it is highly unusual for animals to be running a farm, as long as they continue to withhold taxes and do not attempt to count their chickens as deductions before they're hatched, this department has no cause of action."

The law firm did discover that the mortgage on the farm was held by the Trust US Bank. Payments were up to date, but a few well-placed dollars insured that should a payment be even one day late Biggs would be the first to know about it.

Meanwhile, Mo was learning how to run the farm as a business. While pigs are reputed to be hard workers, it is well known that they often sleep as many as twelve hours a day. Asked about that once, Mo admitted it was true, but explained, "That's only because we don't have much else to do with our time." Certainly that was no longer true. Mo ordered every business text he could find and devoured them. Figuratively, of course. He would read all day and into the night, usually until his wife, Princess, demanded that he come to pen.

Mo discovered there were books covering every conceivable aspect of creating and running a business, from *A Is for Accounting* to *The Insider's Guide to Cashing In on Stock Tips*. Among the books he read were *Leadership Secrets of Attila the Hun* and *Homer Simpson's Management Guide: The What's and Not's of Business*. Some of the lessons certainly could not be applied: "When dealing with strong competitors or those who would cause you to delay your plans," advised *Moving Mountains: The Strategy Secrets of Hannibal,* "the best strategy is to order their heads lopped off and impaled on a stake at least seven feet tall for all who pass to see."

Just about the only business books he refused to order were *Chicken Soup for the Businessman's Soul,* which he felt would be in poor taste and might upset the girls in the henhouse; *Business for Dummies,* because that title made no sense to him; and *Bringing Home the Bacon,* for obvious reasons.

With so many contradictory books each claiming to contain the real secrets of business success, Mo got very confused. "Whoa," he told Lawrence, who would perch quietly on the mantel at night to keep him company, "I never knew doing business was so tough." Finally he ordered copies of *All of Your Business, The Only Guide to Business Books You'll Ever Need* and *The Last Best Book of Business Books, Honestly and Truly the Only Guide to Business Books That You Should Believe,* both of which supposedly explained which business strategy books were accurate. Unfortunately, those two books also contradicted each other.

Mo also sent away for several sets of motivational tapes, which were guaranteed to help anyone increase self-confidence, promote self-assertiveness, and "identify the strongest possible inner you." According to this material, the strongest possible inner Mo was basically ham. While some of this material made sense to Mo, he lost all interest during the "Dress for Success" seminar tapes, which warned specifically against wearing earth tones. Or, as he interpreted that, dirt.

After reading all these books Mo admittedly was even more confused. Every author wrote with great authority that if the reader followed his or her advice success would be assured. So based on all this material, Mo wrote down certain conclusions:

1. Without question, the most important thing for any business is to establish a good firm ethical policy. And if that isn't it, then definitely it is quality control. Or marketing and delivery systems, or maybe a continuing commitment to research and development.

2. A company can only be as successful as the quality of its management. But if the management isn't very good then it can only be as successful as the loyalty of its workers.

3. With proper training, all employees can become equally competent. Except for those employees who will always be superior to others.

4. According to years of research, the single most important factor in job satisfaction to a worker is his or her salary. Or maybe working conditions. Or benefits. Or job security. Or respect. Or something else.

5. A successful manager will treat all of those people working for him exactly the same, spending approximately an equal amount of time with each

one. Either that or a successful manager will focus on his most productive people.

6. The more opportunity employees have for advancement and promotion the better they will do their jobs. Or competition for advancement creates an unhealthy unsupportive atmosphere and leads to unproductive employees.

7. Any bright employee who really desires a specific job will be able to do that job. Or different individuals have different skills suited for different situations.

8. Customers or clients are willing to pay more for quality. Or the key to continued success is low prices.

9. The value of the company's stock can be increased by issuing unrealistically optimistic quarterly projections. Or the value of the stock can be increased by issuing unrealistically pessimistic quarterly projections—then beating them.

10. There is only one best way to work with employees: Treat them all the same. Or the best way to work with employees is to use a different strategy for each individual.

Everyone on the farm agreed that Mo was doing something very important in the "main office," as they had begun to refer to the Goode house, even if no one was sure exactly what he was doing. But soon it became known that Mo was working on "the business plan." Everyone spoke with great respect and confidence about "the business plan." In the mornings many of the animals would stand around the water trough and discuss it, although no one dared admit that they had never seen a business plan or knew what it was. In fact, when one of the chickens said casually, "I forget, what's a business plan again?" everyone laughed at her.

Belle, one of the older sheep, explained patiently, "It's a plan for business, dear."

Lionel Engine, the small but feisty mouse, boasted, "Business plans are very good. I've eaten several of them in my time."

The truth was that very few of them were actually concerned about this plan. Mo was working hard on it, and they trusted him completely. And Mo understood things that were too complex for them to comprehend. He had seniority. They were mostly concerned about having their own needs fulfilled; so long as they got the same feed as every other member of their species and had a warm place to sleep at night they weren't interested in the details of this business plan.

While they waited for Mo to reveal it, everyone went about their daily chores without complaint. In the chicken coop, the forty-eight hens continued to lay their eggs on a regular basis. On a nice warm day they would produce nearly three dozen eggs. Most of the chickens enjoyed their work. They were expected to lay an egg only four or five days a week. While the pay was indeed chicken feed, the job itself wasn't difficult. It consisted pretty much of sitting around waiting all day, interrupted by a few minutes of really hard labor.

The coop was sort of like a large sorority house with feathers, complete with egg-laying cliques. Clara and her best friends Lizzie and Cindy had long squatted on the top shelf, a perch from which they might look down upon all the others. Which they did. The three of them would cluck away all day. And one of their favorite topics of conversation was Rocky "Red" Rooster.

No one on the entire farm complained more than Clara. It was said about her that she wasn't happy unless she wasn't happy. Clara was the kind of hen who would complain because she didn't have teeth, but if she had them she'd complain about cavities. Nothing was good enough for her. Nothing. Her nest was too cold or too hot, her allergies always bothered her, causing her beak to get stuffed up, her feathers were molting, the roots of her comb were showing. But more than anything else, she liked to complain about Red Rooster. As far as Clara was concerned the word "cocky" did not even begin to accurately describe him. "The way he struts around all day with his beak stuck up in the air," she complained. "He really thinks he rules the roost."

Sometimes, admittedly, she said things like that primarily to ruffle Cindy's feathers. It was no secret that Cindy had a tremendous crush on him. She made it so obvious that behind her tail some of the others referred to her as "over easy." But Cindy didn't care what others thought; she was certain she was in love. "He's the only one for me," she willingly admitted, a fact of life on the farm with which no one could logically disagree. When Clara reminded Cindy, as she did often, that he was not the type of rooster to ever settle down, that he was constantly seeing other hens, Cindy defended him by pointing out, "He can't help it, it's his job."

Lizzie was the most independent of all the hens, as well as the best egg producer. Proudly, she laid her eggs without any help from "Mr. Big Shot Red Rooster," making her, as she explained defiantly, "an independent producer." At night, when the other hens huddled together, some of them noted that she had never shown the slightest interest in any rooster. Lizzie paid no attention to the gossip, but she was pretty outspoken about the way Cindy threw herself at Red. "Listen to me," she said, "Red is an idiot." Then she did her well-known imitation of him, which almost always caused the other hens to cackle, "Cock-a-doodle-*duh,* cock-a-doodle *duhhhhhhh.*"

The "Milky Way," as the cow barn was known, was a much quieter place than the coop. The four cows, named by Farmer Goode, in an unusual burst of whimsy, Joan, Paula, Georgina, and Ringolette, took themselves and their work quite seriously. They were only too aware that cows generally did not enjoy the same level of respect as many other animals. Horses were strong, dogs were loyal, cats were clever, cows were . . . cows. Nobody had ever made a movie in which a cow was the hero. Throughout history cows had most often been portrayed as lazy, fearful, moody—that's why they spoke moo—and not very bright; a small, unsophisticated town was called a "cow town," for example, and a person lacking courage was a "coward." This, they believed, was terribly unfair.

Cows didn't kid themselves. They were fully aware of their physical limitations: They were ponderously slow, they couldn't jump an inch off the ground, and perhaps most important, they had no natural defensive weapons. They didn't have sharp teeth or claws. They couldn't even exude a poison like a snake or an insect, they didn't have quills like a porcupine. Cows couldn't run, they were too big to hide, and they couldn't really put up much of a fight. Worse, they were a popular dish.

What cows had to offer were a good brain and a charitable nature. A lot of people mistakenly interpreted their generous nature as stupidity, but cows were smart enough to recognize their own value. They knew that the milk they delivered by the gallon was almost essential for human children, and they knew humans would do anything for their kids. So they gave freely of their milk without the slightest complaint.

On the night Mo had taken charge the cows had said nothing, which as usual was seen as a lack of interest or even understanding. But the cows were using their simple, time-tested survival strategy: Cows are unusually cunning. Smart enough to keep all their emotions concealed. Cows never made a commitment until they knew for certain which side of the barn the sun warmed in the morning. Their loyalty was pretty much limited to their own survival and prosperity. So until they knew for certain what Mo intended to do and how it would affect them, they waited, and watched, and said not a word.

Of all the animals on the farm, the sheep were probably the least concerned about all the changes—which surprised no one. Sheep rarely bothered to think for themselves. They were natural followers. They would admit without embarrassment that the only thing at which they were best was following. In the animal kingdom, when it came to being second, they were always first.

And when just about everyone was talking about the movie *Silence of the Lambs,* Jesse was quoted as saying, "Well, if you had the brains of a lamb you wouldn't have anything to say either." That was the closest thing to a joke Jesse had ever been known to make.

About the only thing sheep truly cared about was their appearance. You couldn't get them past a mirror with a German shepherd. Even Mary, who was considerably overweight, wore thick cola-bottle glasses, and wore her wool in an avant-garde bouffant, just couldn't help admiring her reflection.

Sheep had a natural talent for growing hair, and they would spend hours admiring their reflection in the pond. When Mo needed a receptionist Lily was the obvious choice. Unlike her sister, Lily was as sweet as a lamb is supposed to be. Working as the receptionist required her to look nice, be pleasant to visitors, and follow instructions. Mostly it allowed her to sit at her desk and play with her hair. It was a job for which she was perfectly suited and thoroughly enjoyed.

So whatever Mo decided was going to be just fine with the sheep.

The horse couple, Jesse and Queenie, might have been Mo's strongest supporters. They were both hard-working no-nonsense animals—blue-bridle workers, who said little and gave their loyal support to whoever was in charge. Clara had once cruelly described them as "carousel horses, but without the personality." At work they did most of the heavy labor; they pulled the wagons in the fields and did whatever heavy lifting was required. When doors got stuck they pulled them open. When a tree fell across the road they pulled it out of the way. In payment, they expected to be treated exactly the same as everyone else, although Jesse never said neigh to an extra feed-bag once in a while.

Of all the workers on the old Goode Farm, without any doubt the most nervous about the coming change was Scarecrow.

Everybody else on the place had at least one companion with whom to share their anxieties, but not Scarecrow. Scarecrow was alone, just as he'd been his whole life. As long as he could remember he'd lived by himself, worked alone in his field, and spent his nights alone. He often told himself that he didn't really mind it—and factually that was true because in the traditional sense he really didn't have a mind—but there were many days and nights when he longed for companionship.

Ironically, the only actual relationship with another living being he had was with his longtime enemy, Chucky T. Crow. The two of them had been battling for years, and had gotten to know each other's strengths and weaknesses. Long ago their fights had ceased being about the theft of a few seeds or scraps. Now it was a test of their very natures. Across the centuries the fight for supremacy between scarecrow and crow had been waged countless times in countless fields around the world—without a clear victor. Scarecrow and Chucky the Crow were proudly carrying on an ancient feud.

Each day Scarecrow would stand defiantly in the middle of his field, dressed to scare, waiting and watching for even the slightest clue that the crow was about to launch yet another attack. But Chucky was wily and had learned a lot about the art of subterfuge and misdirection through the years. And almost every day that attack would come without caws, only to be met and blunted by Scarecrow.

For the first few years of their relationship they never spoke. But late one afternoon, after Scarecrow had successfully thwarted another foray, Chucky sat on a telephone wire and asked with frustration, "Hey, pal, what is it with you? What possible difference can a few seeds make to you?"

"You talking to me?" a surprised Scarecrow asked. It was unusual enough that anyone would speak directly to him while he was working. But Crow himself?

"No, I'm talking to that invisible worm. You see anybody else around? Of course I'm speaking to you."

Once Scarecrow got over the initial shock he told the crow that it was a very difficult question to answer. "It's not the seeds, it's my job. I do it the only way I know how to do it."

"You ever think that maybe you shouldn't take it so seriously?" Chucky suggested. "Let's be honest here, standing alone in the middle of a field in all kinds of weather every single day of the year isn't exactly the greatest job in the world."

Scarecrow looked up at him. "It isn't?" he said. That thought had never occurred to him before. Standing there was what he did. He literally was made for that job. And as everybody on the farm recognized, he was extraordinarily good at it. No one could stand still in a field for hours doing absolutely nothing as well as he did.

"No," Chucky replied, "trust me here, it isn't. You know, it is possible for you to move up in the world. You don't have to do this same job forever. You can try another field, if you know what I mean."

That there might be more to the world then protecting this field on the Goode Farm had never occurred to Scarecrow. He knew what he was, he knew his capabilities—but on the other paw, he also knew he had been wrong on occasion and it was possible he was wrong about that. And if he was right that he was wrong, then maybe, just maybe he could do another job. A job with other people nearby that he could talk to, a job that earned him the respect of the animals! "I don't think so," he finally said. "Besides, if I did, who would protect the field from you?"

"'Crow," Chucky said, "sweetheart baby, standing in a field all day scaring birds is not exactly a job that requires a lot of . . ." He paused here, searching for exactly the right word, and found it: ". . . breathing, for example. Pretty much anybody could do it."

Scarecrow refused to believe that. That couldn't be true. And then he remembered that Chucky had a plan of his own: Get the seeds. All this talk was probably just part of Crow's secret plan. "What do you really mean?" he asked suspiciously.

"I been thinking. You know, maybe you and I could work out some kind of deal," Chucky suggested. "Don't you listen to the news? You're spending way too much time in the sun. It's not good for you. When you get older it's gonna ruin your . . . your . . . believe me it's not good for you. So here's what I'm proposing: You go sit down in the shade somewhere, maybe even take a nice nap, and I take a couplea seeds. But just a few, you know, no more than I really need, not so much anybody'll even notice. That way we both get something out of it."

Scarecrow would not even consider it. "I'm a scarecrow," he said proudly. "That's not just a title, that's who I am, through and through. I wouldn't know how to do anything differently."

And so their battles continued. But about everything other than protecting his field, it was agreed that

Scarecrow had nerves of straw. He worried about everything. He worried about the weather and the crops, he worried about the health of other animals. When Chucky was late or went away on vacation without singing a good-bye note he even worried about him. When he had nothing to worry about he worried that something must be very wrong if he had nothing to worry about. So the change on the farm gave him more to worry about than ever before.

With the change in management would he keep his job? Did he still have it, was he as scary as he'd been in the past? Would they make him wear one of those fancy uniforms with his name stitched above the breast pocket? There was nothing for Scarecrow to do but stand in the field and wait. Fortunately, that was his special talent.

But he never forgot that first conversation with Chucky. Was there really another job—a better job— he could do? The seed had been planted and, like the wheat he protected, it began growing straight and tall.

And so, everyone from the mouse Lionel Engine to Beau the Bull simply continued doing their jobs and waited for Mo to announce the business plan.

THREE

Standing upright on his hindquarters, his front hooves leaning on a table for support, Mo stood an impressive five feet tall. He'd found one of Farmer Goode's old wool cardigans hanging in a closet and decided to wear it—but only after receiving permission from the sheep. And while it really was too small for him, most of the sheep thought it was quite flattering. "It makes him look a little like Babe," one of them remarked.

All the sheep immediately agreed, although to sheep all pigs looked alike, so they generally felt that every pig looked like Babe. Actually, Mo was much bigger and rounder than Babe, and his lack of sleep had left deep pouches under his eyes. But as the comparison was meant to be complimentary he saw no reason to disagree with them.

"Animals," screeched Rocky "Red" Rooster, "hereeeeee's Mo." Due to his ability to project his voice louder than anyone else on the farm, Mo had appointed Rooster his new Director of Communications.

"Thank you, Red," Mo said, banging a hoof on the table. "Thank you. Please, would everybody just keep it down for a few minutes." The barn was even more crowded than it had been for the last meeting, so crowded that a swarm of mosquitoes in the hayloft were squashed together. Mo was finally going to present the business plan.

"As everybody knows, for the last few weeks I've been working on our new business plan," Mo began. He grasped a thick pile of paper and held it up high enough for everyone to see. "And here it is. But before I start explaining it to you I want you to know that it's not anything like Farmer Goode's plans."

"What'd he say?" the cow Joan asked Paula.

"I think he said it's not a Goode plan," Paula replied.

Overhearing that, Clara said loudly, "I knew it. I knew it was going to be a bad plan."

"What?" Abe said quite loudly. "And that should surprise you? Whattya think, all of a sudden from a pig you're going to get filet mignon?"

The rumor spread through the barn like visiting locusts: The plan is no good. The plan is a failure. The plan isn't going to work. We're all going to be put out to pasture.

"Hold it," Mo screamed. "Just hold on for a minute."

Following orders, the sheep immediately began looking for something to hold on to.

"Listen to me, everybody," he shouted. "I did not say it was a bad business plan. What I said was that it was not another Goode plan. Don't you understand? It's a no-brainer."

For the next few minutes the animals were on the verge of panic. The plan they were depending on was a failure. Up in the rafters, the old owl Lawrence, unwilling to look at this scene, covered his eyes with his wing. But then, from the dark corner where he had been standing, Scarecrow stepped forward. "Excuse me, everybody," he said politely, "could you please listen." In the dozen years Scarecrow had worked on the farm he had never spoken in public. The sight of him standing in front of the room trying to speak was so unexpected that the barn quickly quieted down.

Everyone stared at him, waiting for him to speak. "See," he said finally, "Mo"—he pointed to Mo—"Mo said it was a no-brainer. So I just thought, you know, that he was talking about me." Several animals laughed, although Scarecrow did not understand why. So he smiled at them with his lipless mouth. "Why don't we just let Mo finish speaking?"

Red screeched again, "Heeeeeerrreee's Mo!"

Mo glared at Red. Then began again. "What I meant to say is that this isn't . . ." He stopped and carefully considered his choice of words. Finally he said flatly, "I'm happy to say that this is a great plan. Not good, great!"

"It's a great plan," several sheep said to each other, quite relieved to hear it themselves. "It's a great plan."

As Mo began speaking, Scarecrow quietly went back to the corner. No one noticed that he was still so nervous that his straw was shaking. But as he faded into the background a feeling he couldn't identify came over him. It wasn't so much that he felt good or bad. Rather, he just felt. And he liked it. He liked it a lot.

Mo explained, "I've read so many books about business and management that I didn't know where to begin. This is our farm, but it's really our business. And if we want to continue living here together we have to start running it like a business. Basically, that means that we have to earn more money than we spend."

Beau thought about that for a few seconds, then asked politely, "Um, please Mo, not so fast."

"Our business," Mo continued, "this farm, is just like any other business. The best way to start getting organized is to think of it as three completely different areas. Each of those areas has different responsibilities. The first area is called administration. That's everybody who makes sure the business runs smoothly. That includes facilities management, animal resources, finance, hiring and firing, training, janitorial services . . ." Mo paused and looked down his long snout at the other animals.

They were all standing absolutely still, their mouths and beaks hanging wide open in amazement. None of them had ever truly believed they actually would have to take complete responsibility for the farm. Farmer Goode had always done that for them. All the things that needed to be done just got done. Broken things got fixed. There was heat in the winter. When someone got sick Old Doc Disney, the one-legged veterinarian, paid a barn call. Hiring? Nobody got hired, they just got born into the job. Firing? Nobody ever got fired. Once in a while Ma Goode would fry a chicken—nobody they knew, of course—but no animal was ever fired. Fried yes, fired no.

Mo cleared his throat and continued, "The second area of responsibility is operations. That's manufacturing and production. That's where so many of you are doing such a great job right now. This is where we make the things that we sell, the products that enable us to earn more money than we need to spend. That includes eggs." He paused and looked at the chickens. "That's you girls," and in response they cackled delightedly. "That's also the milk, wheat, and anything else we can produce here—even honey if the bees are looking for some kind of permanent work." It was well known that bees were hard workers but not very reliable.

Mo continued. "That also includes R&D, research and development. That's where we're going to be designing new products. So if any of you have any great ideas . . ."

Several animals laughed—but not Joan. Mo continued, explaining the importance of production, but she was no longer listening to him. Instead, she was thinking about an idea that had come to her one day long ago while she was eating grass in the meadow. She had never told anyone about it, afraid that they would ridicule her.

But Mo had asked for ideas for new products. She'd heard him. In her mind, she could see exactly what it would look like. Not only would everybody love it, but it would mark the beginning of a new image for cows. "The hobby cow," she thought proudly. Other animals had toys made in their image, teddy bears, chocolate bunny rabbits, stuffed sheep, but never cows. Until now. In her head she saw an adorable little hobby cow in front of a grocery store that boys and girls would want to climb on, grab the reins, and go for a nice little ride. She would tell Mo about it later.

". . . so let me know what you come up with," Mo continued. "Now, the third area of responsibility is sales and marketing. That's the key to our success. Salesanimals are going to determine whether our business survives or"—he looked out upon a sea of very nervous faces—"or survives really, really well."

Finally, many of the animals broke into smiles.

"Then we have our Advertising and Public Relations Departments. For those of you who don't know what that means, Advertising uses pictures and slogans to make people aware of our products and tries to convince them that they should go out and buy them. Public Relations makes people feel good about out products . . ."

Pictures? Georgina thought, instantly visualizing

herself on the front of a milk carton. They'll certainly need a model—a pretty young cow, perhaps? She sighed, and sucked in her stomachs.

"Those are the three major components of our business. All of you," and as Mo said this he swept his front leg across the whole room just as he had seen the politicans do, "will find your proper place in one of those areas. Any questions so far?"

A Dalmatian named Sparky raised his paw. "How do we know where we belong?"

"Good question." Mo looked up into the rafters. "Did everybody hear Sparky's question?" The barn was buzzing. "Would somebody in the back ask the bees to keep it down just a little, please?" he said. When the buzzing subsided, Mo repeated the question, then replied, "Animals are just like people: You can scare them into working hard. You can really frighten workers by threatening to take away their benefits, lower their pay, or even sell them to the butcher . . ."

Every living thing in the barn was stunned into silence.

"Believe me, studies show that no poultry works harder than a turkey the second week in November." Mo knew he'd made his point.

"But we don't believe in doing that," he continued, his voice rising. "What we believe is that animals have earned the right to live long and happy lives. We all know that on farms around the world animals have been enslaved and abused. We've worked our tails off and have never seen any of the rewards. But that's not the way we're going to do business on this farm. One thing my reading has convinced me of is that a happy animal is a productive worker. So it's management's job to make sure you're happy with your job. One way to do that is to help you find the job that you really enjoy, then make sure you have the skills you need to do it well. Because if you really want to do it, you can!"

Scarecrow was confused. Happy? Being happy was a concept he had never even considered. Happy? What did happy feel like? he wondered. Was it different from wet? Would a different job make him that? Truthfully, since that first conversation with Chucky he'd been wondering if just maybe there really was another job he could do. He would need new clothes to be properly suited for any other job, of course, and he might have to comb his mop differently, but maybe it was possible. Maybe Chucky was right, he admitted to himself, maybe there was more to life on the farm than being a scarecrow. Maybe he could be happy, whatever happy was.

He wasn't the only one to wonder about Mo's speech. A handsome young pig whose given name was Aristotle, but who aspired to a career in show business and so insisted on being called by his stage name, Piggy Banks, asked aloud, "So, Mo Man, how do we know which job is the right job for us?"

"According to what I've read," Mo replied, "we start by finding out exactly where we are."

Beau brightened. Finally, there was a question he could answer. "We're right here!" he said firmly.

Mo smiled, wrinkling his snout. "Beau, I don't mean where we are," he explained. "What I mean is, where are we?"

"Ahhhh," Beau said agreeably, having absolutely no idea what Mo was talking about. These changes were all very confusing for him, but he knew that Mo had big seniority, he had experience, so whatever he said must be right. Whatever it meant.

"What I mean," Mo explained, "is where we are as a business. Most of those business books agree that running a business successfully is really simple. Only one thing makes it complicated: people. If you could just eliminate people, businesses would have a lot fewer problems . . ."

Wow, Joan thought, what a great idea. If you really could eliminate all the people, animals would have a lot fewer problems too.

"But we can't do that. What we can do is make work more comfortable for our animals. To do that, though, the first thing we really need is to find out how you feel."

Abe shook his head. "You had to ask?" he said loudly. "You want to know, okay, I'll tell you, but it shouldn't happen to you. There's this pain in my lower back that when I bend to pick up . . ."

"Well," added Henrietta the Chicken, "I have morning sickness pretty much every morning."

"No, no, no," Mo said rapidly, "not how you feel, how you feel. What you think about the way things are going on the farm. We're going to conduct what's called an 'animal opinion survey.' That'll tell us where we all stand on things . . ."

No one on the farm had ever participated in a real survey, so Mo had to explain the process to them. "You just answer a few pages of questions about everything on the farm. It's just a way of finding out what you're thinking."

Joan answered for many of the animals when she said, "I'll tell you what I'm thinking. I'm thinking I don't want to take this survey."

When Clara heard Mo describe the survey as "pages of questions," she got very nervous. "Is this like a test?" she asked.

"What?" Jesse said. "This is a test?" His ears straightened in memory of the last test he'd taken. He could still feel the pain. Doc Disney had stuck a long needle deep into his backside and withdrawn at least two gallons of blood—maybe three.

"No," Mo said, "no, no, it's not a test. It's nothing like a test. The questions don't have right or wrong answers. We just want to know how you feel about things."

"I don't like needles," Jesse said. "They hurt. That's how I feel."

"There are no needles, Jess, I promise you," Mo continued, beginning to get just a little frustrated. "Look, everybody. We're just getting started. What we need to find out is what you're good at and what you like to do."

"Oh, I can tell you that right now," Mary said. "I'm not good at surveys and I don't like to do them."

"Long as there're no needles," Jesse said, pretty much to himself. "I don't like needles."

Mo took a deep breath. "All right, okay, after the survey we want to find out if you're doing the right job—the job that matches up with your skills. We do that with what we call competencies. That's just a business way of figuring out what skills it takes to do a specific job . . ."

Way up in the rafters, the leader of the Hawks, a tough pigeon named Squash, shifted uneasily. "Hey, Homey," he said to the pigeon perched next to him, "you getting all this?"

Homey turned his head almost completely upside down. "Hey, look at me. Do I look like a parrot to you?"

"Don't you go getting smart with me," Squash warned him. Squash slicked back his wing and let out a low whistle. It was a tough job running a gang of birdbrains.

"Hey, Squash, how long you known me?" Homey asked. "Believe you me, the one thing you don't got to worry about is me getting smart. This is as good as it's gonna get."

Squash nodded toward Mo. "I don't like this, not at all. Trust me kid, change is never good for the pigeons. That's why we like statues. All right, here's what I want you to do. 'Member where old man Biggs's office is . . ." Seconds later, unnoticed, Homey pushed off the rafter, made one broad sweep of the barn, and flew out the hayloft window.

"The third thing we're going to do," Mo explained, "is focus on your personal development. We want to help you grow . . ."

Lionel Engine's ears perked up. Grow? Did Mo really say grow? Lionel Engine found it difficult to believe that Mo had learned all of this complicated business stuff from books. Personally, he liked things simple: You put the key in the ignition and the engine starts. Simple. But he decided right then and there that if business books could really make you grow, he was definitely going to start eating more of them.

Mo continued, "The way we help you grow is through a process called a 360-degree review. That's where we ask questions about you to all the animals around you. A 360 allows each of you to be rated, or judged, by all the animals you work with . . ."

The moment Beau heard Mo say he was going to be "judged" his heart started pounding. That was the one thing he feared. Unlike his father and great-grandfather, he wasn't perfect. His forelock was gnarled. The judges would see that immediately. He would be embarrassed in front of all the other animals.

". . . a long series of questions, then several interviews . . ."

When Mo finished, Jesse raised his tail. He really had only one question. "Are there any needles in the 360s?"

"No needles, I promise," Mo said. "Some of you are

probably wondering what we use these 360s for. Simple. All of the jobs on the farm can be divided into two general categories," he continued. He realized that he was giving them a lot more information than most of them would be able to remember or understand, but he felt it was important to introduce the broad concepts. "And those are management and labor. Basically, managers help workers do the best job possible. The managers make the policy and tell labor what to do and then provide them with whatever they need to do their job . . ."

Jesse nuzzled Queenie. "That's like us, sweetheart. You're the manager, I'm the labor."

"Oh, Jesse," she said, but he noticed that she was blushing.

". . . Some of you are wondering, I'm pretty sure, how you become a manager or when you work in labor . . ."

Henrietta the Chicken clucked to herself. There was nothing Mo could tell her about being in labor. She was in labor just about every day.

"Based on the results of the 360s, we'll figure out who will make the best managers and who should be doing exactly what jobs . . ." Mo continued explaining the purpose and use of these 360 reviews for several minutes. "But I want you to understand something. Where you start isn't necessarily where you finish. You can start at one job and, if you do well at it, then you can get a different job—a job that pays even more. In business, this is called climbing the ladder of success."

The ladder of success? Lionel Engine didn't like the sound of that at all. Many months earlier, when he was just a little squeaker, Spike the Cat had cornered him in the wheat silo. Lionel figured pretty quickly that his best chance to escape was to climb the wooden ladder to the safety of the loft. He leaped as high as he could and managed to grasp the lowest rung. He whirled himself around in a complete circle as if he were on a gymnastics high bar. He picked up speed and flung himself into the air grasping for the second rung—and missed it completely. Instead he slammed into the wall, where he lay, stunned, waiting for Spike to pounce.

Incredibly, somewhere in the distance a dog started barking. Spike was momentarily distracted, enabling Lionel to scurry across the floor and dive into the safety of a pile of hay. Subsequently he'd spoken to Spike twice, not that it was possible to have any kind of intelligent conversation with a cat, but neither time had Spike brought up the encounter. Lionel saw no reason to mention it. But from that encounter he had learned an important lesson: Ladders are not designed for mice. It was an important thing to know. He would not be climbing the ladder of success. So he knew that he would have to find another means of clawing to the top.

It had been a long meeting, but Mo had even more to tell them. And this part, he knew, would be the most difficult to explain. "Every single one of us on this farm," he began, "mammal, poultry, rodent, insect, and strawperson, whatever your species, beliefs, or gross weight, whether you're a man, woman, or it, have exactly the same rights. There's nothing that can ever change that. We all have equal rights, and we all have the right to grow equally! We can all be as good as we can be!"

Lawrence ruffled his feathers in agreement. For someone who was not an owl, Mo occasionally showed signs of great wisdom.

"In the old Goode days, we never got a real chance to grow. We never had the chance to find our inner animal. Who knows how great each of us might be if we were allowed to really spread our wings . . ."

Beau was pretty sure he understood what Mo was talking about until that last sentence. He could grow, he knew that for sure, having gained almost 120 pounds in the last year alone, but spread his wings?

Mo continued. ". . . When Farmer Goode was in charge we all worked very hard, we did our jobs, and what did we get for it?" He paused, listening for an answer. There were a few murmurs, but otherwise silence. "That's exactly right," he said finally, "pretty much nothing. Food and shelter, that's it. We did most of the work, and he got paid for it. Well, those days are over." He raised his voice and promised loudly, "Did you hear me, those days are over! From now on everybody is going to get paid for the work that they do!"

The barn erupted in cheers. "Yeah!" Rocky "Red" Rooster crowed. "Yeah! We're gonna get paid! We're gonna get paid!"

The loud cheering continued—until Belle asked sheepishly, "What's paid?"

The cheering gradually subsided until only one voice could be heard. "Yeah!" Rocky "Red" Rooster shouted happily. "What's paid?"

"Well," Mo began explaining, "paid is what you get in return for doing your job. It's an amount of money. You get it every week and it's called a salary."

"Celery!" Paula said with surprise, her tail wagging. "Oh, I love celery." She turned to her sister Georgina. "We're getting paid celery."

"Salary," Mo corrected. "It's a salary, not celery."

"Oh," Paula said, her tail dropping straight down, "well, is it as good as celery?"

"It's not food," he tried to explain, "it's money—dollars and cents. You can use it to buy food or anything else you want." Suddenly he had an inspired thought. "Paula, you can use your salary to buy celery!"

Paula was still confused. "I don't understand, Mo," she admitted. "If you can't eat it, why does it have a scent?"

"A cent," Mo said, getting frustrated. "It's not a scent, it's a cent."

Paula turned around. "I'm going to my stall and chew my cud. This business is too complicated for me." And as she pushed her way through the crowd she continued muttering, "Salary. Celery. Scent. Cent. I don't understand business at all."

One of the chickens asked, "Mo, how much paid do we get for our job?"

"That depends on your job. And your job is determined by your 360 review. And it's not *paid*, it's called *pay*. You get paid your pay." Here it comes, thought Mo. "But the thing is, everybody's pay is different. Each job pays a different salary. So the amount you get paid depends on the job that you do. Everybody got it?"

Joan asked the question that was on everybody's mind: "Who gets paid the most?"

"That depends on the job," Mo replied. "That's why we're going to do the survey and the 360s. But remember, if you do your job well, you can move up to a better-paying job."

Joan did not like that answer. She said to Paula and Georgina, "Sure, right. Sounds like the same old 'screw the cows' to me."

"That's fair," Jesse agreed in his deep voice, "everybody should get paid according to their specific job— just as long as horses get paid exactly the same pay as everybody else."

Suddenly voices erupted all over the room. It was pretty obvious that nobody really understood the concept of salary, but everybody had a strong opinion about it. Mo called for order and was completely ignored. For the first time since the animals had taken charge of the Goode Farm, the situation threatened to rage out of control.

Mo banged and banged his hoof on the table until the barn finally quieted down. "Wait a second," he screamed at everyone. "Let me finish. There's more to it than that. There are other things we all get in addition to salary. Benefits, they're called. That means annual vacation time, overtime pay, health insurance, paid maternity leave, child care . . ."

Maternity leave? Clara looked at the other girls in astonishment. Maternity leave? The possibility of such a thing had never occurred to her. But the other chickens were looking in a completely different direction. She followed their gaze across the room—all of them were staring intently at Rocky "Red" Rooster. And truthfully, she admitted to herself for the first time, he was looking pretty good.

". . . but the most important benefit is the fact that we all own this farm equally. Farmer Goode gave it to all of us. So what we're going to do is issue shares of stock in the farm. And every one of us will get the same amount of stock."

Almost everyone in the barn was dumbfounded. Stock? The only thing they knew about stock was that that's what they were. According to what Mo was saying, they were going to own themselves. But didn't they already own themselves? They had been in business only a few weeks and already business was too confusing to understand.

All except for Clara, who had paid little attention to Mo's final words. Instead she was focused completely on Red. She had never noticed before how much the narrow comb on top of his head looked like a very fashionable mohawk.

FOUR

Scarecrow scratched his straw head. The question read: *Do you have any physical handicaps that would prevent you from performing certain tasks?* The form then noted in boldface print that federal government guidelines prohibited any employer from discriminating against an employee because of such a handicap.

So with great trepidation, Scarecrow bravely checked the box marked "yes." And in the blank space following the instruction, *Please list all such handicaps,* he carefully printed, "No brain." This was a very difficult thing for him to admit, but if Mo was telling the truth, his lack of a brain would not hurt his opportunity for success.

Like everyone else on the farm, Scarecrow had been dreading this day. For the previous week it had been just about the only topic of conversation. Mo had tried to calm their fears, emphasizing, "Stop worrying, this isn't a test. It has nothing to do with intelligence. It's just going to help us understand our business. The only thing these surveys will tell us," he explained over and over, "is what you like and don't like."

"That's the problem," Beau said sadly. "I don't like taking surveys."

Mo emphasized that they were not competing against anyone else. Everyone accepted that completely, then just about everyone set out to prove that they were the most noncompetitive of all. In particular the cows did everything possible to show that they were more noncompetitive than the horses. They spent much of their time in the pasture, telling everybody who passed that they were very busy not even thinking about the survey. But sometimes they couldn't help but ask how much Jesse and Queenie were not talking about the survey.

Of all the residents on the farm, the only one who had even come close to taking a survey before was Lily. While working in the farmhouse she'd found an old copy of *Cosmopolitan*, which included the story "How to Tell if He Thinks You're Hot!" It required her to answer fifty questions about herself, which seemed very close to the way Mo had described his survey.

According to her score, Lily most definitely was hot. But to her disappointment, no one was interested in the results of this particular survey. What they really wanted to know was how it felt to take a survey. Lily was barraged with questions about it all week—from everyone except the cows, who pointedly told her several times they were not asking her questions about what it felt like to take a survey.

On a cool Saturday morning everyone on the farm gathered in the barnyard to begin answering the 150 questions on the survey. As they began just about the only one who was not nervous was Rocky "Red" Rooster, who was quite secure knowing he was Director of Communications. In fact, the only question that caused him even slight hesitation was *How many children do you have?* After some deep thought he wrote: "Thousands (approx)."

Everyone else struggled: Even the most basic demographic questions caused considerable confusion. The dogs, for example, were not certain what scale they should use to answer the question *Age?*

For Lionel Engine and the rest of the field mice the real difficulty was just completing the survey. It took them a great deal of time to crawl from question to question. Lionel didn't know some of the answers, and had to estimate his height at "2.4 inches" and weight at "11.3 ounces." As he wrote down his weight he was reminded he'd been eating a little too well recently and probably needed to drop a quarter-ounce.

Ringolette decided no one would be hurt if she was not quite accurate in answering that weight question. So she scribbled in "445 pounds," then covered her paper so Joan couldn't see her answer. Beau proudly wrote "1,834.6 pounds" in that space. Beau had always taken great satisfaction in being a lot of bull.

The 150 questions covered a variety of aspects of life and work on the farm. Having never conducted a survey before, Mo initially believed he could simply use a standard form. In one of his books he found several sample surveys. The first one had been given to applicants at a major law firm. One of the first questions asked: *You have been hired by the CEO of a Wall Street firm accused of insider trading. Is your first response a) order the new luxury sedan, b) install an in-ground swimming pool, c) plan a vacation, d) all of the above.*

Obviously that survey could not be applied to the farm. Then Mo found one that had been prepared for appliance repairpersons. It began, *When taking this survey you must respond to all the questions a) tomorrow, I promise, b) soon as the answers I've ordered get here, c) when Joe gets back to the office, d) when the cow jumps over the moon.* After briefly considering this survey, Mo realized it would not work either.

Finally Mo realized he had to create a survey specifically for the farm. To do that—as instructed by his business books—he began by organizing focus groups. These were informal interspecies gatherings to discuss the concerns of everyone living on the farm and help decide what questions should be asked on the survey.

Many of the issues were predictable: For example, just about everyone wanted to talk about food and shelter, the selection of managers, benefits, security, Mr. Biggs, and the future of the farm. But other subjects were less predictable: For example, there was some question whether a certain unnamed mouse was using steroids. At least one individual suggested that several of the underemployed local squirrels be hired to manage the crop storage facilities. Someone wanted to know if the farm had a policy of discriminating against fish. There were suggestions that at least some of the cows be convinced to give chocolate milk, that research be done to determine how to get additional horsepower from Jesse, and that it be made mandatory that the rabbits take anger-management courses.

The 150-question survey was the result of issues raised in these focus groups. The questions in the first half of the survey focused on how the farm was being run. This included questions like:

Do you enjoy getting up at dawn? (Y or N.)

Would you prefer to wake up to recorded music rather than a live rooster?

Do you like the well water currently available in the trough or would you prefer carbonated mineral water? (Circle one.)

How would you describe the decor of your current residence? a) modernistic, b) eggclectic, c) bow-house.

How would you describe your sleeping quarters? a) too hard, b) too soft, c) just right.

If we had a cafeteria, what type of cuisine would you

like? a) oats and bran, b) Chinese, c) Italian, d) garbage.

If you are currently working in production (eggs, wool, milk, crops), have you ever experienced separation anxiety? (Y or N.)

How would you rate the job being done by the CEO and President Mo? a) good, b) very good, c) terrific.

Do you think the cows are getting the respect they deserve? a) Y, b) N, c) Who cares? d) c.

Questions on the second half of the survey were designed to help "Mo-nagement," as some of the animals had begun referring to those animals running the farm, determine how to plan for the future. These questions included:

What recreational facilities would you like to see built on the farm? a) ice-skating rink, b) bowling alley, c) volleyball court, d) pole vaulting run and pit.

Do you believe the Kentucky Derby discriminates against animals other than horses? (Y or N.)

Which of the following would you like to see added to the farm first? a) satellite television, b) French hair salon, c) onsite daycare, d) Starbucks.

At a barn dance, do you believe animals should be permitted to dance standing up? (Y or N.) If you answered yes, should hippity-hoppity music be permitted? (Y or N.)

What do you believe is the biggest problem currently facing the farm? a) world peace, b) economic upheaval, c) Ed Biggs, d) fleas.

How best would you describe human beings? a) everywhere, b) loud, c) controlling, d) tasteless.

Several of the animals struggled through the survey. Clara and the rest of the girls in the coop encountered an embarrassing situation when forced to respond to the question *If you were a food, what food would you be?*

Abe the Goat was moving rapidly through the first part of the survey until he reached the question *Do you feel there is too much pressure placed on your job performance?* For reasons he couldn't explain, that question bothered him so much that he picked up his survey booklet and ate it.

Reluctantly, Lawrence gave Abe another copy, and warned him that they didn't have any more copies to waste. Abe pointed out that it wouldn't become waste for several more hours, and even then it would actually be fertilizer.

While everyone on the farm was busy with the survey, in the nearby city other events were transpiring that would eventually affect them all. Following Squash's orders, Homey had arranged a meeting with Mr. Biggs. "Have a seat," Biggs offered in his most friendly tone, patting a stool on which the pigeon alighted. "Perhaps you'd care for a dropper of water?"

"Nah," Homey said, then explained why Squash had sent him. A deal, he said, that would be of interest to all concerned. As Biggs listened intently, Homey explained that the Hawks had an aerial observation system covering the entire Goode Farm. "We're all over the place," he said. "We can watch every move they make and they don't even realize what's going on. It's perfect."

"I see," Biggs said, nodding. "Very interesting. And you're telling me this because . . ." His voice trailed off innocently.

"Come on, Biggs. We know you want the land to put up strip malls."

Biggs raised his eyebrows in surprise. "Oh. You do, do you? And may I ask how you came upon that information?"

Homey's attempt to cackle instead came out as a low whistle, ruining the effect completely. Undeterred, he explained, "Let's just say a little birdie told me."

Biggs smiled. "And let us say, for argument's sake, that this 'little birdie' was correct. If I understand you, what you are proposing is . . . agricultural espionage?"

Homey replied, "Call it whatever you want. We prefer to think of it as a competitive advantage. Look, you and Squash, you're like . . . birds of a feather . . . well, except you. Anyway, Squash told me you'd understand that in business . . ." he continued, intending to point out how important it is to know exactly what your competitor is doing. Unfortunately, before he could make that point, a little dropping landed on the cushion.

Ignoring it completely, Biggs said, "And in return for this information?"

Homey shrugged his wings. "A warm wire to sit on in the winter . . ." He paused, stared right at Biggs, and said flatly, "And all the kernels of corn the gang can eat."

"You drive a hard bargain, my fine-feathered friend. But I think we have a deal." Biggs sighed, desperately trying to hide his glee. The pigeon, it turned out, was a pigeon.

Back on the farm, it was generally agreed that taking the survey was a lot easier than most had expected, except for having to answer all those questions. But no one seemed to have suffered any permanent injuries and some of the more self-confident animals were already talking confidently about taking the next survey. The questions that caused the most conversation were those focusing on recreational facilities that might be added to the farm. Recreational facilities had been limited to radio and watching crops grow. Lionel Engine was particularly excited about the possibility of an ice rink, having dreamed about being on skates since seeing an ad for Disney's *Mice on Ice*. And Beau couldn't wait to go bowling, although he wondered if he could find a 160-pound ball to fit his hoof.

Mo, his newly appointed Executive Vice-President, Lawrence the Owl, and their several assistants spent more than a week sorting through the results of the survey. What surprised them most of all was the fact that many of the animals actually expected that the information gathered from the survey would be used to make changes on the farm. "They definitely didn't understand the purpose of this survey." Lawrence sighed. "Maybe we should explain to them that all we wanted to know was what we don't know."

"It was the most important survey we ever did," Mo said flatly. The question arose what to do with the results of the survey. Lawrence suggested that the survey results be filed in the Very Important Documents file. Everyone agreed enthusiastically; unfortunately no one could remember where that file had been filed. So instead, the results were safely stored under a pile of yellowing *Farm Management* magazines.

The next step in the reorganization was to figure out the talents needed to do each job on the farm and then determine who would best fill those jobs. In one of his business books, Mo read that the best way to do that was to interview the top performers in each job area to determine exactly which qualities allowed them to rise above all others. "Well, that's pretty easy," Lawrence said, when Mo explained it to him, "my wings."

"Everybody's a comedian," Mo had responded. Then he explained to Lawrence that he was referring to "competencies," the traits that apparently made someone particularly good at a specific job. The theory seemed to be that if you could figure out the reasons one employee was especially good at a certain job, then other employees could learn how to do the same things and also excel at that job.

So in the weeks following the survey the Executive Committee interviewed the so-called "best in breed" from each area of the farm, trying to determine what made them good at their jobs. "So Joan," Mo asked, "what do you think enables you to give seven gallons of milk every day?"

This was the first time Joan had ever been inside the farmhouse. Just being there made her so excited she paid little attention to the questions. "I don't know. I just squeeze," she admitted, then confided, "I guess I'm very good at squeezing."

"Superior muscle control," Lawrence noted.

"But what do you do that's different from the other girls," Mo asked, "that enables you to give more milk than they do? I mean, where does all that milk come from?"

"Oh, that's easy," she said. "See, each night before I go to my straw I make sure I drink a lot of milk."

Lawrence asked Jesse about his great strength: "Do you think it's just natural or do you have to focus on what you're doing?"

"Definitely!" Jesse said, quite intimidated but trying hard to be helpful. "I just naturally focus on what I'm doing."

Mo asked Scarecrow where he'd gotten his remarkable ability to stand in the field all day. "Everybody else would need to sit down once in a while. You never do. How come?"

"I don't really have a choice," Scarecrow admitted. "I don't have knees."

Lawrence wrote down, "Needs knees."

Mo was not surprised to discover that few animals had followed well-thought-out strategies for success. Among the exceptions was Henrietta, who was among the farm's top egg producers every year. "It's simple," she explained. "There's this mental technique I use. I concentrate hard as I can on the desired outcome. And then it comes out."

From these interviews, Mo developed a list of the behaviors that seemed to show up most often among the top performers. The list included almost fifty different traits and techniques, although in fact none of the animals personally used more than four or five. But to Mo the logic was clear—the more of these "competencies" an employee exhibited the more chance for success. These competencies included:

- The ability to sleep standing up.
- The ability to concentrate on a specific task without being distracted by telephone calls, e-mails, or flies.
- Patience—to be able to sit quietly for hours.
- Endurance—particularly the ability to run at a good pace for a prolonged period.
- Advanced tail control—global swatting ability.
- Exceptional leadership and command talents—especially as exhibited by Big Sam the Sheepdog, who excelled at barking orders.
- The ability to focus complete attention on a single

task without losing effectiveness—or, as several animals explained, "I don't think I think at all."

While there was still a lot of "Mo-nagement" to be done, the time had come to assign managers to the different areas of the farm. To make these selections Mo and Lawrence took into consideration all the information gathered from the survey, the focus groups and interviews, and the presence of the competency traits. Then, they picked the animals who had been on the farm the longest—the animals with the most seniority. This was based on Lawrence's firm belief that those animals who had been doing a particular job the longest obviously had the most understanding of how the job should be done.

There were, of course, some hurt feelings and damaged egos when these positions were posted. Clara was so upset when Lizzie was made chicken coop manager that she briefly threatened to stage a sit-down strike. That threat failed when Henrietta reminded her that her job consisted of sitting down most of the day, and suggested that Clara consider a stand-up strike. Rather than standing up for her beliefs, which always exhausted her after a few minutes, Clara accepted Lizzie's promotion.

"Oh, Clara," Lizzie told her, "honest, nothing is going to change. We'll still be working right next to each other."

"Oh, all right," Clara said, somewhat relieved.

And then Lizzie added, "It's just that from now on I'll be sitting just a tiny bit higher than you."

To just about everyone's surprise Miles, the most debonair goat on the whole farm, was named manager of the Wool Division. On the farm Miles was known to work hardest at figuring out how not to work hard. And at that he worked very hard, finding all types of ways to convince other animals to do his work. "He always gets the job done, somehow," Mo had explained. "Besides, he's been here almost eight years."

There was also a slight problem when Queenie was promoted to stable manager, which officially made her Jesse's boss. Jesse was to stay in labor. "Oh, it's nothing," she told him reassuringly. "Nothing is going to change at all. Just like always, you'll do whatever you want to do. It's just that first I'll tell you what you want to do. And then you'll do it."

"I don't understand," Jesse said. "We're married. Isn't that the way it's always worked?"

Queenie nodded. "Yes, but now I'll be getting paid extra for it."

Just about everyone agreed that it was appropriate for Abe to be made manager of the Consumer Complaint Department.

The first thing the new managers did was circulate the list of desirable competencies to their workers. These are the things that the most successful animals do, they explained, so the more of these you can do, the more successful you'll be. For many animals, this proved to be quite confusing. Orville the Pigeon, for example, wanted to know why it was so desirable for him to be able to give seven gallons of milk. Lionel Engine knew he had exceptional leadership qualities, but as hard as he tried he couldn't get out a single bark. Lily did not want to be any stronger because muscular girls didn't look very feminine. Big Sam the Sheepdog had beautiful tail movement, but each time he tried to flap his forelegs he collapsed onto his chin.

No one was expected to possess all of these competencies, the managers explained. But with training and practice everyone should be able to master a few more of them. Lionel Engine believed that, and walked around for several days trying to learn how to bark. Instead of "bow-wow," the sound that came out was an unfortunate "mew-mew."

As Mo was determined to apply the latest management techniques, the final thing he did before assigning jobs was conduct 360 reviews. "This is an opportunity to find out exactly how we think about each other," he said cheerily. "It's a chance for all of us to . . ."

In his mind, Abe finished the sentence for him: ". . . get even." And he couldn't help but smile, a great big goat smile. There was a good reason he'd been born an animal.

". . . identify our weaknesses so we can work on them." Mo explained how the 360s worked: Each animal was rated by everyone around him—coworkers, managers, even executives—on a specific set of statements. For example, everyone working in the barnyard rated everybody else in the barnyard, and all the animals in the pasture rated each other. The results were supposed to provide a strong indication of how well each animal was doing on the job, emphasizing both strengths and weaknesses.

The statements for this 360 came from a variety of sources. Some of them were selected from sample 360s, others were based on the focus groups and the competency list, and others were left anonymously in the barn suggestion box.

The individual filling out the forms either agreed or disagreed with each statement strongly or moderately. The statements were pretty straightforward. They included:

- Uses humor effectively.
- Shares his lunch on a daily basis.
- Has the ability to eat through clutter.
- Thinks she's better than anybody else.
- Contributes to group projects.
- Is sympathetic to the needs of others.
- Rarely makes embarrassing noises in public.
- His or her bark is worse than his or her bite.
- Contributes eggs willingly.
- Exhibits compassion and animanity.
- Has a bad temper.
- Has had distemper.
- Can handle problems that crop up.
- Knows when to say yea or neigh.
- Can handle problems with crops.

- Has good mechanical skills.
- Works well with others.
- Builds a good nest.
- Sticks his snout into other animals' business.

As Lily and Mary walked back to the barn after dropping off their completed forms, Lily said softly, "Mary, can I ask you a question?"

"What's that, dearie?" Mary responded.

"There's one thing I don't understand. I mean, I know I'm not very smart or anything . . ."

"C'm'on, you're perfectly adeq—"

"No, no, don't rooster me, I know the truth. We've had all these surveys and interviews and focus groups and we filled out all these forms, but the one thing nobody ever asked was what anybody really gets done—like how many eggs the girls lay in a month, how much milk Joanie gives, how many acres were planted, they haven't asked us a single question about that."

Mary nodded. "What you're talking about is the way they used to do business. You see, Lil, that's why Mo is the Chief Executive Animal and we're not. For example, say Cindy has a great month and lays twenty-six eggs. She just did it. There's no way of being sure that the next month she'll lay another twenty-six eggs. But if she really understood how she did it, if she had mastered all the techniques involved in the process, if she was in a supportive environment, maybe she wouldn't lay twenty-six eggs the next month—but she would know why she didn't. And then each time she didn't make quota they could correct all her mistakes."

"Baa," Lily said, shaking her head in wonder, "it's a good thing we've got Mo in charge to figure out what we need to figure out."

Mary agreed, it was indeed a good thing.

The 360s did yield a tremendous amount of information about all of the animals. For example, the cows were generally more respected for their quiet dignity and dedication than anyone would have suspected. Abe the Goat rated quite poorly on having a sense of humor, although apparently he was considered one of the better dancers on the farm. Big Sam the Sheepdog was perceived as selfish, with a bad temper and the lowest-rated dental hygiene on the farm—even lower than Scarecrow, who didn't have teeth. Scarecrow, it turned out, did not have many friends. He was considered a loner. Most of the chickens felt that the pigs needed to focus on their cleanliness, while, according to the earlier "animal opinion survey," the pigs felt their sty was too clean. Queenie was admired for her caring nature and optimism. And to no one's surprise, Piggy Banks was voted Most Likely to Succeed.

When Mo finally made the job assignments, he told everyone that in addition to the test results, experience, education, natural talents and skills, leadership ability, desire, and the needs of the farm all were part of his decision. Even though Mo explained it that way, and everybody who heard him say it nodded knowingly and felt confident that the best practices of modern management had been applied, that wasn't completely accurate.

The truth was that so much of the collected information had been confusing and contradictory that Mo had finally decided to follow the dictates of the book that advised, "When in doubt, trust your gut instincts." As a result he had decided to keep most animals in their old jobs.

Certainly one of the most perplexing problems he had to resolve was recognizing the difference between his "gut feelings" and common indigestion.

When Rocky "Red" Rooster announced very loudly that their job assignments were posted on the side of the barn, everyone crowded around to see where they would be working. A lot of them were surprised at the results. Almost everybody was already doing precisely what all of these factors indicated they should be doing. And in most cases there was a high degree of satisfaction in doing it. So they were assigned to the jobs they were already doing. For example, the chickens, cows, and sheep were to stay in manufacturing and production. And Mo's three piglets were to continue their custodial work, picking up after everyone. And with one exception, the birds and the mice were assigned to the field.

But that was some big exception. Having scored extremely high in areas of self-confidence, self-control, leadership potential, and especially motivation, Lionel Engine emerged as the best-qualified individual on the entire farm to operate heavy equipment. He was assigned to drive the tractor. Several animals objected to this, pointing out that Engine was a mouse. But the Executive Committee was adamant. They had a pile of test papers taller than . . . taller than Engine himself, actually, that proved statistically that Lionel Engine was more qualified than anyone else for this particular job. "Okay, maybe it doesn't look exactly right," Mo admitted, "but we can't just ignore the results. It's all right here on these papers. If we just did what seemed to make sense, then we'd be free to make any decision we wanted. Then what would happen? Why would we even bother to conduct such extensive surveys and testing if we weren't going to be committed to the results?"

To make it possible for Lionel Engine to drive the tractor, they nailed large wooden blocks to the control pedals and piled phone books on the seat.

"Just gimme the keys," Engine squeaked boldly, "and get out of my way."

Scarecrow slowly and anxiously read each list searching for his name. He hadn't whispered a word to anyone, mostly because he was afraid they would think he was foolish, but he had decided he wanted another job on the farm. He hated to admit it, but Chucky had been right. Scarecrow was wasting his life. Since his first conversation with Chucky he had been thinking, which was something he almost never did. It had never occurred to him before that he didn't have to spend the rest of his life doing this kind of work. He was a scarecrow, proudly doing what scarecrows did. Even when he was thinking, he had to admit that he loved his job. Keeping his field crow-free, protecting the crops, brought him tremendous personal satisfaction.

But what it didn't bring him was respect. That was clear from the results of the 360s. He began to realize that the others on the farm took him for granted. All he was to them was Scarecrow, a scary-looking guy who stood there all day, just another straw man in old torn clothes. So when Mo offered the opportunity for advancement Scarecrow got very excited. It almost didn't matter to him what the new job was, just as long as it earned him respect—and maybe the chance to work alongside someone else, someone to talk with so he didn't have to spend all those hours alone.

Scarecrow sighed deeply. He found his name near the bottom of the Operations list, under "Security Department: Field Security." He was going back to the field, back to the same old job. As he walked away one of the barn cats asked, "So what'd you get?"

Scarecrow shrugged. "Same old, same old," he said as brightly as he could, and then repeated sadly, "Same old, same old."

He was not the only one disappointed with his assignment. Piggy Banks had made it known to everyone how much he wanted to work in media relations. He had a good reason for that. Until a year earlier Aristotle had been very proud of his heritage. His whole life he'd bragged that he came from impressive stock. His great-grandfather had served at the White House. Unfortunately, as Mo finally explained to him, that wasn't quite accurate. In truth, his great-grandfather had *been* served at the White House.

That news had sent him spiraling into a deep depression. It was about that time that he discovered rap music. He fell in love with its message of alienation and disaffection, and knew what he wanted to do with his life. No pig from the sty had ever made it professionally as a rap singer and he believed that he had the goods to break through that barbed-wire barrier. He had all the right credentials to be a rapper: "I pretty much grew up in the pen," he said. Working in media relations would have enabled him to meet the press. And a rap singer who really was a pig had all the hoofmarks of a great story. He just had to find the right reporter and he was on his way.

Unfortunately, he was assigned to the field—semihard labor.

But even in Piggy Banks's wildest dreams he couldn't have imagined the degree of media interest in a farm being run by animals. Biggs had been the source of the initial story, calling the *Tribune* to tell them, "Something very strange is going on out at the old Goode Farm."

The result was an animal-interest story buried in the middle of the newspaper. It included a brief description of the events that led to the animals' gaining control of the farm as well as a description of how it was being run. Mo was quoted as saying, "We intend to run the farm as a profit-making enterprise. By applying the accepted principles of good business management we feel confident we will be very successful."

Had it not been a slow news day this story might have quietly disappeared. Instead, desperate news editors searching for something to fill pages of their own papers pounced upon it. *Animals Taking Over!* headlines blared. *A Beastly Business!* others warned. According to several stories, a local businessman named Biggs pointed out, "This is potentially a very dangerous situation. If this farm succeeds the future of other industries may well be in question."

Television picked up the story. It moved almost immediately from the late-night news to the Sunday-morning political shows, where the meaning of such a dramatic experiment for the future of all mankind was endlessly debated. While one of the participants shouted that this marked the beginning of the end of civilization as it has been known, another one calmly suggested replacing the word "mankind" with the more accurate "allkind."

Mo politely rejected all requests for interviews on the telephone, promising to call back as soon as he had appointed a spokesanimal. But that did not deter an industrious reporter, who brought on his show a sheep-dog that supposedly had worked undercover on the Goode Farm. The "exclusive interview" with this dog failed completely, however, when the dog refused to respond to a single question, and instead began licking his microphone.

The farm was deluged with offers from producers.

An independent network announced plans for a movie in which animals take control of a farm and use it as a base to launch an attack on the nearby village, tentatively titled *The Bad Farm.* Mo also received offers to permit the name of the farm to be used on a wide variety of products, among them soft drinks, deodorants, glue, hair-growing products and hair-removal products, even a musky perfume. He was a little disappointed that no company offered him the opportunity to endorse the one product that might have interested him—old coffee cans full of leftover coffee grinds and melon rinds.

He turned down every offer, explaining, "We need to focus on our business, which is farming." He even turned down a request to appear on David Letterman's show, suggesting that he might be willing to do the show "when Letterman starts doing a segment titled 'Really Smart Independent Animal Tricks.' "

The attention from the general media faded quickly, and the farm became primarily a business story. *The Wall Street Journal* speculated "Is the Farm a Goode Investment?" *Forbes* offered advice on "Protecting Your 401 Canine." But most of the other stories wondered if the farm could survive without the guidance of business professionals.

To the great dismay of Mr. Biggs, who was waiting impatiently for the farm to fail, daily life returned to normal. Each morning Rocky "Red" Rooster woke everyone at sunrise, although his wake-up calls got progressively longer as he began to include reports of news on the farm—"Egg production is up three from yesterday; from the duck pond Dahlia the Duck is proud to announce the birth of six ducklings"—finishing each report by noting it had been "brought to you by Rocky 'Red' Rooster, your friendly farm alarm!"

It took only a few days for everyone to get used to the new structure. Although there was some grumbling about "certain managers, who think their feathers are fluffier than everybody else's," generally the transition went quite well.

The animals had to be creative to figure out how to do some of the jobs that had traditionally been "human" jobs. The fields had to be seeded by ants, with each worker ant carrying a single seed to a designated spot, in exchange for honey produced by resident beehives. And among the several tasks assigned to Beau the Bull was the milk collection. Large milk containers were hung from his horns, like giant earrings, which he carried from the barn to the pasteurization machine.

Sometimes the work was difficult, and many tasks took longer than before, but everyone worked in harmony, believing that somehow Mo would be able to take all the discordant initiatives and somehow blend them into a beautiful rhythm.

FIVE

 Mo had vision. He could see far beyond the Goode Farm. He could see a giant agribusiness, run completely by animals. He could see farms all around the world where animals would be free and safe to grow and reach their fullest potential as nonhuman beings. And while Goode Farm was a fine name for a small, family-owned farm, it was not suitable for the megafarm that would one day become a reality.

And so in anticipation of that day the Goode Farm legally became known as All Animals Agricultural Industries, Incorporated. AAA Industries, Inc.

In other changes, Mo announced that henceforth the "hen house" would be known as the Female Chickens' Residence and, out of respect for the size and industry of ants, "ant hills" would be referred to as "ant mountains." He did, however, at least temporarily turn down Lizzie's request that female managers be called woman-agers.

Mo began the task of transforming the Goode Farm into AAA Industries, Inc. Among the business books that had most influenced his planning was the best-selling *Managing Heaven: St. Peter's Guide to Running Your Business.* According to that book, St. Peter had learned that no one person, with One obvious exception, could successfully run a massive enterprise like Heaven without considerable help. Out of necessity he learned how to delegate authority to managers. His managers worked directly with the angels to make them as productive as possible. Mo realized that the only thing St. Peter's managers had in common with some of his managers was that they had wings and the ability to fly, but he thought the basic advice was pretty sensible. Pick the most experienced managers, give them as much support as they need, and trust them to manage their workers. Or, as it was summed up, *Manage others as you would have them manage you.*

Some of his newly appointed managers tried to make up for their lack of experience and training with enthusiasm. Joan, the new manager of the Milk Production Department, mistakenly decided that being a good manager mostly meant being a great cheerleader. So each morning she would stand next to the production line as it delivered milk, shouting, "C'mon, girls, you can't fail; just keep on giving 'til you fill that pail!"

In the Female Chickens' Residence, Lizzie thought

the best way to increase production was to build team spirit. "Up and on 'em, ladies," she'd shout each morning. "If we work together we can do a lot better than we did yesterday. So let's hear it now, what are we—chickens, or eggs?"

Unfortunately that question always started a lengthy debate that often ended up in a lot of shouting. Henrietta simply refused to believe she had come from an egg, claiming that the pigeons brought her to the farm. The fighting made many of the chickens too nervous to meet their egg quota.

Miles, the suave mountain goat who had been named manager of the Wool Division, enjoyed telling the "little ladies" how he was born in poverty on the side of a mountain in Russia and was imported to America, making him "a truly important goat." Miles was one of those clever goats who believed flattery could accomplish anything. "I was born so close to the stars," he had been known to say, "so I could appreciate your beauty."

The immediate problem he was facing was fashion; short hair was popular and all the girls wanted to bob their hair. "Oh, Lily, my queen of the rocks, instead of cutting off your hair why not just take your scissors and cut directly into my heart, because the result is going to be exactly the same thing."

Lily, of course, was taken with his charm. "Oh, Miles, do you really mean that?"

"Does the full moon not thank the sun for its reflected beauty, my sweet?"

Mary, though, did not as easily succumb to his attempts, telling him, "Listen, you Volgarian, you start that crap with me and I swear they'll be serving your heart as the Tuesday night special at Pete's Tavern."

"Ah, how I love to see that volcano in your heart erupt," Miles said.

"Can it, shish kebab. Flattery doesn't work with me."

In the stable, Queenie had developed her own managerial style. "Jessie, listen to me, please. There are only two ways of doing things, my way or the wrong way, but the choice is yours. And there are two places you can sleep—in the stable with me, or in the barn, but the choice is yours."

The manager of the barn mice was a steel-gray cat named Buck. Buck had long curly whiskers, short hair, and absolutely no sense of humor. Buck believed in managing entirely by intimidation. "I'm the big wedge of cheese and you're the mice," he told them, "and the only thing keeping us apart is a steel bar on the business end of a spring held back by two pounds of pressure. But I'm warning you, you little rodents, if you disappoint me, throngggg!" And then he laughed. It worked. The mice were afraid of him. He would tell them, "I like my mice quiet, hard-working, and medium-well. You keep your tails clean and we'll get along just fine. But if you don't . . . throngggg!" and they would quake in fear and go back to work. Mostly, they just tried to avoid him. When they saw him coming, they would hide. If something went wrong or if they had a problem, they ignored it or tried to cover it up. They were just too frightened to ask the cat-manager for any kind of assistance.

There were at least as many different managerial styles as there were managers. Mo's half-brother, Miney, tried to manage the field workers, among them Scarecrow and Lionel Engine, with reason and friendship. He sat with each of them and reviewed their responsibilities, trying to be understanding and compassionate. "You've got the most important job on the farm," he told Scarecrow, "protecting our crops against those who would destroy them. First thing in the morning you have to be standing there on guard against those birds. Then in the early afternoon you have to stand there, guarding every last seed and plant against birds. And then by late in the day you have to stand there, guarding the crops against—"

"Birds," Scarecrow finished.

"That's right," Miney said. "Let's review it, okay?"

"First I stand there in the morning, then I stand there in the early afternoon, and finally I stand there in the late afternoon," Scarecrow said confidently.

Miney smiled warmly at him. "Are you sure you didn't go to college?"

"No," Scarecrow said softly. "I didn't, but maybe someday . . ."

Then Miney would have a similar conversation with Lionel Engine. "You've got the most important job on the farm," he told him. "Driving the tractor in all kinds of weather, doing all kinds of different jobs—plowing, planting, harvesting—we all depend on you."

"I like to drive fast," Lionel Engine responded.

While some of these managerial strategies were successful with some workers, there certainly was no consistency. The same technique that resulted in one cow giving an extra half-gallon of milk caused another cow to give less milk. In some sections the fields were beautifully planted, in other sections nothing grew but weeds. No matter how many different accounting methods Lawrence used to interpret the ledgers, there definitely was no overall improvement in production. In fact, in certain departments, production actually declined.

"There's a lot of confusion on the farm," Homey reported happily to Ed Biggs. "A lot of the workers don't know what they're supposed to be doing or how they should be doing it. And some of them aren't very good at what they're doing."

"Perhaps you'd like a few more kernels of corn," Biggs responded. And as soon as Homey completed his report and flew away, Biggs would be on the telephone with his bankers, reassuring them that the farm was failing and that the land soon would be his. "Mark my words," he promised, "the next time you see that pig Mo, he'll have an apple in his mouth!"

Mo really didn't know how to solve the problems. But late one night, while he was rereading *Hell on Earth: The Leadership Secrets of Satan,* several paragraphs attracted his attention. "Managers can be the key to creating complete confusion in your workforce. By making certain your employees never know what to expect from their supervisors—even from day to day—you can substantially increase their level of anxiety and frustration and almost guarantee that everyone will be unhappy. Thus you will successfully maintain a very undesirable workplace. The result will be falling production, financial losses, and eventual failure."

The book also pointed out that every ladder goes in two directions—just as some workers will choose to climb up the ladder to success, the right amount of improper planning can be used just as successfully to make them climb down to failure. "The way to create a climate that insures unhappiness and failure is to make certain your managers are climbing down that ladder. Each and every one of the ten rungs on the ladder to failure is important."

- The top rung: Make sure your managers put the wrong people in the right jobs.
- Second rung: Set unrealistic goals that can't be achieved. But if anyone gets too close move the goal line.
- Third rung: Treat every employee exactly the same, no matter what their individual skills and desires.
- Fourth rung: Determine the weaknesses of every employee and make sure they are all doing jobs that emphasize those shortcomings. For example, make sure your shyest people have as much direct contact with your customers as possible.

- Fifth rung: Keep pay and benefits to the absolute minimum—but make sure your employees find out how much more than them other employees are making.

- Sixth rung: Be sure that your employees have every tool and all the materials needed to complete an important assignment—except for one really small and important thing that it will be impossible to obtain.

- Seventh rung: Never overlook an opportunity to undermine your employee's self-confidence. Master several clever remarks that will produce insecurity. For example, "How could you screw that one up? It was so simple even my aunt Beatrice could have done it right—and she's 102 years old and thinks she's a foghorn."

- Eighth rung: When an employee is really good at a job, immediately promote him to a job at which he's not as good.

- Ninth rung: Insist that your workers take training classes that will have absolutely no value in their jobs. For example, make sure production workers have computer programming skills.

- Tenth and last rung on the ladder: Regularly schedule "very important" meetings with workers to review their progress and discuss their future—then cancel at the last minute without giving any reason and tell them, "Ah well, it doesn't matter anyway." Then walk away without saying another word.

As Mo finished reading he let out a long wheeze. "Wow," he said to Lawrence, taking a long drag on his cigar, "you should take a look at this list."

He pushed the book over to Lawrence, who read the list quickly, nodding as he did. "They wouldn't work for us," he decided, "but you got to admit that those rules have worked pretty well for Satan."

Mo was determined to avoid every single one of those mistakes. So the very next day he met with the farm's entire managerial staff to begin establishing general rules for managers. After a long discussion they agreed on the very first rule that they all would follow. Jesse wrote it in white paint on the side of the barn:

1. Any animal can accomplish anything—if you just try hard enough!

Probably the most important thing decided at that first managerial meeting was that the managers would meet with each employee to help him draw up an IDP, an Individual Development Plan, that would help chart a career path. This was a major change on the farm. Until then, planning for the future had pretty much been limited to deciding what to eat for dinner that night.

This was precisely why a few days later Scarecrow found himself meeting with his supervisor, Miney, at the wooden picnic table next to the barn. "Sooo," Miney said, "I guess you don't have an IDP?"

Having no idea what an IDP was, Scarecrow shook

his head and confided in a whisper, "I don't even have any underwear. They didn't give me any."

"An IDP is a plan that you make for your future," Miney explained. "You decide what your career objectives are and the best way to achieve them. Haven't you ever thought about what you want in the future?"

Scarecrow had a ready answer for that question. "Well, I really would like some underwear. And a warm coat too," he said. "Sometimes it gets really cold just standing out there in the field."

"That's not really what I mean," Miney explained gently. "Let me put it this way: Do you really want to spend the rest of your career working in the same field?"

A strange feeling ran through Scarecrow's body. At first he believed it was probably some bug that had gotten lost under his coat and was searching for a way out—that happened a lot—but then he realized it was an emotion. He recognized it. It was the same emotion he'd felt after his conversation with Chucky. Having experienced so few emotions in his life, he couldn't put a name to it, but it was a combination of excitement and fear, with an added dash of anticipation and just maybe a tiny little hint of happiness. He'd spent his entire life working in the same field. He knew every square inch of dirt. He knew how the shadows moved on September afternoons. And now he knew for certain that he wanted to know what life was like in other fields. "I'd like . . ." he began, but it was very hard for

him to force the words out of his mouth. "I'd like . . .
to be in a different . . . field."

There. He'd said it. He waited, almost afraid to take
a breath. But nothing happened. The world didn't end.
The barn didn't fall on him. He nodded his head,
slowly at first, then faster, gaining confidence, and finally he repeated, "I'd like to work in a different field."

"Okay," Miney said casually, as if Scarecrow had not
just risked his very existence. "It's good to have ambi-
tion. You got any idea what kind of field you might
like?"

Because the entire concept of thinking was new for
Scarecrow, he didn't have the slightest idea how to
imagine his future. So he didn't know how to answer
the question.

After an uncomfortable minute of complete silence,
Miney tried to direct him. "It helps if you list the
things that you're good at. And then list those things
that are important to you in a job." Again he waited.
Again, Scarecrow was silent. "So what do you think
you do best?" Miney asked.

"Waiting," Scarecrow said.

"You mean you have a lot of patience," Miney trans-
lated into a meaningful business term.

"Watching," Scarecrow said. "I watch really carefully."

"Good at details." Miney wrote it all down. "Let me
ask you this," he said. "If there was one thing, only one
thing, that you could change about your present position, what would that be?"

That was an easy question for Scarecrow to answer. "I would like to sit down. But I don't have any knees."

"Okay. Anything else you'd change if you could?"

Scarecrow said it would be nice if he had someone to talk with at work.

"Let's see," Miney mumbled to himself, leafing through pages of job descriptions, "a job that requires a lot of patience, someone who's good at details, and is done sitting down. Preferably with others. Hmmm." Then he sighed. He sniffled slowly. Finally, he said, "Ahhhh, here's something that would be perfect for you."

As Scarecrow's eyes were buttons he couldn't actually open them any wider, but he did raise his pasted-on eyebrows in anticipation.

And Miney said, "Have you ever considered going into production?"

Production? Scarecrow recognized that word. He didn't know exactly what it meant, although he had heard Mo use it several times. But if it was in a different field and he could sit down and have someone to talk to, it might be something he would enjoy. "That would be very nice," he agreed.

"Well," Miney said, writing it all down on Scarecrow's IDP, "I have to be honest, it isn't going to be that easy for you. According to the results of the 360s, you've got an awful lot to learn. See . . ." Miney showed him a clipboard with rows of meaningless numbers on it. "Pretty much everyone agrees you've mastered 'standing up for extended periods.' That's what this five is right here. But when it comes to sitting down . . ." He paused. "It's not something you're really good at, is it? You scored a little less than a one."

Scarecrow admitted "sitting down for extended periods" was not one of his talents. But he was confident that with some assistance, he could master it.

"Maybe," Miney agreed, "but you're definitely going to have to take some training classes. If you can get that score up to even a three that'd be fine. It's just a matter of growing . . ."

Scarecrow wondered about that. He had never heard of anyone growing knees.

"But there's no question about it," Miney said flatly, "by doing such a great job in your present position, you've earned the right to be considered for a different job. You've got a perfect attendance record, you protect your field, and there hasn't been a single complaint about your work." He smiled, as he completed filling out Scarecrow's IDP. "I'd hate to lose a good worker like you, but if that's what you really want, let's see if we can make it happen for you."

Managers held similar meetings with just about every worker on the farm—with varied results. In Milk Production, for example, Joan told each member of her group, "I want you to forget all about cow hide, from now on it's going to be cow pride! We're cows, we can do anything. Think Cow Power!"

But as she discovered, most of the cows were content. They enjoyed their work, although there was a consensus that they'd like to open a little later in the morning. And generally they were satisfied with their working conditions. It bothered Joan that they were not more ambitious, that not one of them showed much interest in moving into Operations—where the key decisions were made. "I mean, do you really want to be taken care of your whole life?" she asked them. "Are you really satisfied having absolutely no responsibilities except to give milk every morning? Is it enough for you just to have grass to eat and fields to roam?"

Well, yes, every cow in her department agreed, absolutely. As long as nobody knew how smart cows really were, Paula told her, there was no pressure on them. They had nothing to worry about. They lived a carefree existence. That's why cows come home when they want to—not when someone else tells them it's time. But if it ever became known that cows actually were very bright, they would be forced to get involved in all types of activities. Instead of enjoying their freedom, they would have to spend their time going to meetings, reading reports, and making decisions. Other animals would start depending on them. They would be asked to settle disputes, which would cause them to develop enemies. Suddenly they would have things to worry about. "Being a cow is like being a member of a wonderful secret club," Paula concluded, "so please don't give away our secret."

The only thing she would like, Ringolette admitted, was a workout stall in the barn. Just a heavy-duty treadmill, she said, and a ballet bar. "Maybe you noticed that I'm not as round as I used to be. I used to be a perfect 154-154-154," she added somewhat sadly. "I'd like to get my shape back."

Joan sighed, "Don't you see," she said, "you're still living back in the Goode days. You need to take control of your future, you need to develop and grow." She opened her genuine plastic briefcase and took out several thick reports. "I've spent a great deal of time going over these IDPs," she continued, "and look here, look how low the whole group scored in stamina. We rated a one. We can do better than that, we're cows! So from now on we're going to start off each day with a group jog." Her voice grew with excitement. "Before you know it, Ring, you're gonna be back in good shape. Just one lap around the whole farm each morning, and soon we'll all have the stamina we need to succeed!"

The chickens expressed quite a variety of dreams in their IDPs. Some of the girls were excited about the opportunity to earn more than chicken feed. Cindy told Lizzie she hoped to work in Corporate Communications. Of course she does, Henrietta clucked. "And I'll bet I know who she wants to communciate with, not to mention any names—Red Rooster."

Clara was particularly nervous about her IDP. Not quite understanding what it was, she was afraid to commit to any answers that could possibly affect her future. For example, she told Lizzie that her "short-term goal" was "to make no long-term goals." So when Lizzie asked her to describe her "long-term goals" Clara was able to respond, happily, "None. See, I'm fulfilling my short-term goal."

Trying to make Clara understand the potential value of a well-thought-out IDP, Lizzie asked nicely, "Clara, dear, don't you want to get ahead?"

"Why?" Clara responded defensively. "What's the matter with the one I've got?"

Mary took her IDP very seriously. Mary had plans. She had no intention of spending the rest of her life on the farm working as a living Chia Pet. Why should she have to give up her beautiful hair to keep a human warm? What did a human ever give her—besides "Mary had a little lamb"?

Mary was determined to develop her skills. More than anything else, she realized, numbers had always interested her. She liked mathematics. It was well known that all over the world, people lay awake counting sheep, so why shouldn't there be at least one sheep who liked to count? The Accounting Department, she decided, that's where she wanted to work. With hard work, perseverance and a little luck, someday she might even become the farm's comptroller.

When Miles read Mary's IDP his thick wool curled. Mountain goats were known for their upward mobility, and his own career, he knew, depended on his ability to motivate his flock to grow hair, and Mary was a natural. She was born to grow long beautiful wool hair, and Miles did not want to lose her. "But Mary, my delicious little lamb . . ."

"Oh, just stop it, Miles," she said, "and I'm not your little lamb. Technically, in fact, I'm a ewe."

Miles chuckled seductively. "No, no, my fine four-footed feline," he protested. "See, I'm me and you're you. Me," he said, pointing to himself, which was physically a very difficult thing for a goat to do. "You," he continued, pointing at her. "But if you're saying that you would like me and you to be us, it would be my pleasure, my little baa-bee."

"No, no, no, horns-for-brains, not you, ewe. *Ewe,*" she repeated slowly, emphasizing the word. "Do you even know what a ewe is?"

"Absolutely," he replied confidently. "I am the manager. I'm in charge! I bring you together. I herd you."

Mary paused and looked around curiously. There was no one else nearby. "Excuse me? You heard what? What did you hear?"

"All the workers in my department. That is my job. I herd you, all of you."

With that Mary finally accepted the fact that any manager crazy enough to hear voices was not prepared to help her progress in the company. She stood up and walked proudly out the door, one foot after another foot after another foot after another foot.

Lily was a much more traditional sheep. She was happy to follow instructions, thrilled to do what she was told—as long as she looked good doing it. It was Mo, who worked with her every day, who saw her potential for personal growth and urged her to consider pursuing other positions on the farm. "But I don't want to," she protested. "I like being the receptionist."

"At least think about it," he said, "that's all." But whether or not she did so, Mo was determined to see her succeed. And he would make sure it happened.

In the stable, Queenie urged Jesse to complete his IDP. "Let's look at these questions. First, what do you consider your strengths?"

"I'm strong," he replied honestly. She waited for him to elaborate. Wanting very much not to disappoint her, and having pretty much exhausted all the correct answers to that question, he finally added, "And I'm good at running in big circles."

But she wrote down on his IDP form, "I thoroughly enjoy reading classic literature and working on my computer. I am looking for an intellectual challenge."

Jesse smiled sweetly and said those words she so enjoyed hearing: "Anything you say, dear."

The cat, Buck, believed the entire concept of IDPs for his department was ridiculous. They're mice, he thought. All the hard work and training in the world can't turn them into cats. Rats maybe, he decided, not completely sure that rats weren't just mice who worked out a lot. But he dutifully met with each mouse in his department.

To his surprise, he discovered that mice were responsible and ambitious. As one of his workers, Mickey the 5,234,000th, told him, "I've got 352 kids to support. I need this job." Although Buck had a difficult time recognizing each of his workers—to cats most mice look alike—he actually found himself starting to like some of them. And when the mice conquered their fear that Buck was just looking for a midnight snack, they realized he was a reasonably decent cat. So the forms got filled out and Buck ended up admitting to his workers, "Remember 'throngggg'? Just kidding."

The only animal on the entire farm who refused to fill out his IDP was Abe. He told Mo, "When I was just a little kid, my father warned me, 'Don't ever tell them nothing,' he said. 'Be your own goat.' Of course, then he met some cutie patootie and I never saw him again. But I never forgot that advice. You're a nice pig, Mo, and thank you very much for your pretty forms, but please, just leave me to be my own goat."

SIX

Piggy Banks rapped:

You can put your charm right back in da barn,
'Cuz there ain't no way to keep this pig on your farm.
My name is Piggy and if you think I'm fakin',
Just go ahead and try to put your paws on my bacon.

They gave this farm to the an-ni-mal,
From Clara the Chicken to Beau the Bull.
Said turn it in to a business deal,
Or else you end up as a Big Mac meal.

'Cuz my name is Piggy and I'm telling it true,
If you want to start a biz here's what ya gotta do.
Best you let your animals do their thing,
You know the fish gotta swim, and this pig gotta sing.

Yo! Take some advice from this hip-hop pig,
Let your very own workers find their very own gig;
If they need some help give a hoof and a arm,
And that's how you keep 'em down on the farm.

The barn erupted into cheers as Piggy Banks completed his first public performance. Although he had some difficulty scratching the turntables with his hooves, everyone agreed he was amazing. "Just imagine," Paula said as the cows strolled back to the barn, "if a pig could make it as a rapper, then anything is possible for animals."

"Maybe," Georgina agreed. "As long as no one expects *me* to jump over the moon."

Truthfully, the animals paid more attention to the rapper than his rap. For many weeks now, Mo had been trying to reinforce his belief that with hard work and dedication—when given the opportunity and support—all animals could become whatever they wanted to be. Maybe Georgina couldn't actually jump over the moon, but as Joan pointed out, Georgina could be put in a rocket, shot into space, and circle the moon.

Although no one could see the benefits of cows in space.

The highlight of the gathering was the unveiling of

the second rule that Mo directed to be painted on the side of the barn. In large white letters it read:

2. Don't settle for second beast.

When it was unveiled it was met with complete silence. No one minded being referred to as a beast. They knew it meant the same as being an animal. But most of them just didn't understand what the rule meant. So Mo explained that it meant simply—don't be satisfied doing the same old job. Whether he or she has fur or feathers, no matter how many legs or wings he or she has, every worker on the farm has the right to be promoted to a better job—as long as he or she is willing to work hard for it.

"That's right," Lionel Engine agreed as he casually tried to adjust the utility belt from which hung several full-sized tools. He had started dragging it around in an effort to appear more mousculine. Unfortunately, even when buckled to the very last hole, the belt fit him only slightly better than the equator would fit around a beach ball. So whenever he moved he would have to spend substantial time pulling it along, so mostly he just sat inside it.

Engine's attempt to look impressive by carrying more than he could manage served as a good metaphor for the farm. To the outside world it looked as if the transition to an animal-run farm had gone smoothly. But on the farm serious problems had arisen. In his quest to make the farm an efficient business, Mo had sometimes overlooked the fact that the business was being a farm.

As long as everyone remained satisfied doing their natural jobs, there had been only minor problems. In the past, no animal had known that change was possible. They accepted their fate without complaining, just as animals had done throughout history. It had taken Mo and the Executive Committee several months to convince them that their lives could be better—that a job didn't have to be drudgery, that options existed, that they had the right, and the ability, to make choices that would make their lives more enjoyable. Cows didn't have to give their milk, they had that choice! Gradually, the animals began to accept the fact that wonderful possibilities existed. And that was when the problems began.

The animals knew that things weren't running as smoothly as once they had—that was as obvious as the barn door that no longer could be shut tightly—but they believed that Mo had a plan, and that eventually it would work. Besides, many things had changed for the much better. For example, they had learned they had rights that governed their workplace. They could determine the rules by which they would work together. For example, the chickens decided that no one should wear too much perfume.

As others began to accept the fact that they had the right to make choices in their workplace, they began to use them, admittedly with the caution of chickens crossing a newly paved superhighway. Or at least they tried to use them, sometimes without understanding what they meant. For example, Ringolette decided she would like to sleep later in the morning, so she officially requested the right to cyber-commute. "I want to do my job on a computer. All I need is the computer and lessons to learn how to work it."

This went all the way up to Mo, who had to explain patiently that some jobs had to be done in the office. Especially jobs in the Production Department.

The rabbits, believing they had discovered a loophole in the benefits package, began filing requests for maternity leaves. As the average gestation period of a rabbit is approximately thirty-one days, and maternity leaves lasted two months, it was clear there was a serious problem. Fortunately, it was solved when Mo pointed out that the rabbits were not full-time farm workers, but rather independent contractors, and thus did not qualify for the benefits package.

Some requests were a bit more complicated. The girls in the Female Chickens' Residence wanted new ergonomic work stations. Something, they suggested, that after a long day of sitting would be substantially more comfortable than a few pieces of straw.

Nobody knew how to solve the problem. An Italian designer had created a high-tech minimalist nest made of leather and aluminum, but while it looked fabulous, all the hens agreed it also looked as if it would be extremely uncomfortable. Particularly on cold mornings. Very little work had been done to bring the nest into the twenty-first century. The girls were asked to list the elements that would compose the perfect nest, maybe even do some sketches, and told that Animal Resources would try to find someone to fabricate it. While it was not a solution to the problem, at least it was an acknowledgment that a problem existed. And, maybe most important, somebody was interested in solving it.

Problems continued to show up unexpectedly. One afternoon the newest problem arrived carrying a clipboard and a pile of warning notices. He was, he explained officiously to Mo, the designated representative of the United States Department of Labor, Division of Child Labor. Mo was very impressed, as he'd never before spoken with a representative of the entire United States government, and the representative responded that he had never had a conversation with a pig, although he did not seem as impressed. He told Mo that the government had been informed by a person or persons unnamed that the farm was utilizing child labor, which was certainly illegal. Should these heinous charges be proven, he warned, the result could be the imposition of terrible penalties. Those penalties could lead to the shutting down of the business and the sale at auction of all its assets.

Everyone on the farm knew that the unnamed person or persons was Mr. Biggs. They were absolutely right. Biggs had filed an official complaint alleging that many of the workers on the farm were under the legal working age of sixteen. Sure, Mo admitted, that was true. In fact, he added, two of his own kids were less than a year old and working every day. The representative was shocked—until Mo pointed out that he himself was only seven and he was President and Chief Executive Animal. "Truthfully, though, most of the animals here call me the Chairman of the Boars." Mo waited for a laugh that never came. "Chairman of the Boars," he repeated, "pigs . . . boars?"

"I see," said the representative of the entire government sternly. "So it appears that we do have a problem."

Mo pointed out that animal ages are calculated differently than human ages. For example, seven human years was about the equivalent of thirty pig years. Dogs' and cats' ages were seven times human years. "And mice," Mo said, shaking his head, "no one knows how to calculate mouse years. And besides, mice usually lie about their age."

The representative admitted that this was indeed an unusual problem. He would have to speak with other representatives of the entire government of the United States to determine how to proceed. And then Lily showed him to the door frame.

The moment the government representative left, Mo began worrying. This was the ultimate takeover threat. The government could take over the farm, and then Biggs would undoubtedly purchase the property. At times like this, Mo had difficulty deciding who was the real pig.

And while Mo didn't say a word about his fears to anybody, at night when he and Lawrence were hard at work he wondered aloud if the animals would be considered part of the farm "property." "If Biggs ever gets control of us . . ." Mo didn't even have to finish that sentence. Lawrence fluttered his wings as a chill filled the room. But there was nothing they could do except wait for the government to tell everyone on the farm how old they were.

Early one morning soon afterward, Rocky "Red" Rooster announced, "Milk production is off four gallons, and AAA Industries, Inc., is pleased to announce that training classes in many fascinating and important subjects begin today. Times and places will be posted on the barn. This message has been brought to you compliments of Zooommm Cola. Remember, when you need energy fast just say 'Ummmmm Zooommm.' This is Rocky 'Red' Rooster, your friendly farm alarm, saying, Have a good day."

The training classes were designed to try to combat diminishing production in almost all areas of the farm. Everyone agreed that everyone was trying to do the best job possible, and Mo was faithfully following the concepts explained in his books, but the results continued to be poor. More instruction, Lawrence advised. The more animals knew the easier it would be for them to correct their weaknesses. Mo agreed that training would be the key to saving the farm.

Initially, thirty-five classes were offered. A few of the courses offered general information—such as reading, animal history, computer programming, and a course intended to improve personal relationships called Animal Husbandry. But most of the courses were intended to provide the animals the basic skills they needed to improve in their current jobs, or advance to other jobs and executive training.

This was all in coordination with Mo's stated belief that everyone should be "the best animal possible." It was extremely important, he had said, that each animal be well rounded—which naturally led to some jokes about Ringolette being "too well rounded." "For the future of this farm," he explained, "every one of us needs to learn how to do several different jobs. The truth is that each of you can be anything you want to be . . ."

"Oh, good," Ringolette thought. "I definitely want to be thinner."

". . . if you're willing to work for it. If you're willing to try hard enough." Mo suggested that each animal take another look at the list of desirable competencies and use them as a guide to pick a training course. These courses included Enhancing Self-Esteem, Conflict Resolution—Closing the Barn Door Theory of Compromise, Diversity in Action—Scents and Non-Scents, Muzzle Thyself—How to Control Your Inner Animal, and Business and Negligence Law—Biting the Hand That Feeds You.

Scarecrow immediately signed up for Laying Up on the Job—Techniques of Egg Production. Mary signed up for two courses, Accounting 101 Plus 102 and Calculating Women—Female Accountants in History. Even Chucky signed up for a course, Introduction to Security, which was more commonly known as Wait Training. Initially, Lily failed to sign up for any courses, but at Mo's urging she finally agreed to take Phone-ethics—Selling Wire to Wire.

Scarecrow was very excited about his course. It was, he believed, the first step toward his new career. The course lasted three months, meeting two nights a week. Taught by experienced chickens, it covered everything from the Theory and Technique of Egg Laying to Secrets of the Egg-Laying Professionals. Most of the students in the course were young chickens and ducks or older poultry taking a refresher course. While they had natural ability, nobody worked harder than Scarecrow. Having to overcome the handicap of being created without knees, he practiced the bending postures for hours at a time. It was incredibly hard work, but he stuck with it, hour after hour, day after day.

Amazingly, his hard work paid off. He figured out that by bending and twisting from the waist he could sit down. He also worked on strengthening the stomach muscles necessary to push out an egg, he spent many nights warming a wooden egg, and he did all the suggested visualizations. He was a dedicated, motivated student, acing all the written tests. In fact, he was the best student in the class. In fact, the only thing he didn't do was actually lay an egg. But he remained optimistic that someday he would lay an egg. He wanted to do it so much, and he worked at it much too hard not to be able to do it. If Mo was right, if anyone could be anything they wanted to be if they just tried hard enough—he would lay that egg.

Many students did well in their classes. Most of the

sheep, for example, easily mastered Accelerated Hair Growth. And Jesse registered for a motivational course in which he actually did very well—when he bothered to attend class. It was not a course he really wanted to take. One night, in the stall with Queenie, he admitted that he was taking it only because, he said, "I feel a lot of pressure to succeed."

"Oh, Jesse, that's ridiculous," Queenie replied lovingly. "It doesn't make the slightest difference to me if you become a Vice-President or just a Senior Supervising Manager. I just want you to be happy."

"But I am happy," he said, "right now. I really like my job. It's interesting to me. I like when I get up in the morning not knowing if I'm going to be pulling or pushing that day."

Queenie understood. "Then that's really what matters, isn't it? Since you know what you like, I think it's really important that you"—she smiled—"that you be your own horse. Don't you pay any attention to things other people tell you. Make your own decisions."

"You're absolutely right, dear," Jesse said, "I'm going to make all my own decisions—just like you tell me."

But not all the trainees mastered their classes. Lily just wasn't interested in learning how to become a strong leader. Didn't anybody notice, she wondered, that she was a sheep, not a sheepdog? She wasn't interested in turning her baa into a bark. She was very happy doing what she was told, except when they told her that she should do what she wanted to do. That was what she *didn't* want to do, and she didn't want to tell anybody else what to do either. She liked being one of the herd.

But Mo had insisted that she take a leadership course. You have great potential, he told her, so she went to the classes and did her barnwork. And secretly she thought she was wasting her time. If I ever become a leader, she promised herself, the first thing I'm going to do is eliminate leadership courses.

Nobody loved their training classes more than Lionel Engine. He was easily the best student in engine repair, perhaps because no one could get inside an engine better than he could. Lionel continued to amaze everyone on the farm who had ever doubted that a mouse could successfully drive a tractor. On a daily basis he was proving that his physical shortcoming—he was considered both height- and length-challenged—could be overcome with determination, creativity, telephone books, and, when it was needed, strong support from others to deal with his weaknesses. In fact, he had gotten so good behind the wheel that instead of plowing the fields in nice straight furrows as they did on other farms, Lionel Engine actually preferred to write his full name in script in the furrows.

As much as anyone else on the farm, Lionel had benefited from the Management Assistance Program. In conjunction with the training classes, managers in each department started working directly with their employees to analyze their performance in their current jobs. It had taken several months to get this part of the program operating, mostly because the managers lacked experience and had to learn how to manage. While some succeeded, like Lionel, many of them failed and had to be replaced. There was, for example, that dreadful incident between Buck and one of the mice working in his department.

It started as a discussion between Buck and a mouse named Whitey Cheesenabber about the use of personal days, and had escalated into an argument that ended, unfortunately, when Buck temporarily forgot all the confrontational techniques he'd learned in workshop and ate Whitey. Throughout business history many executives have been known to "bite the heads off" of subordinates for infractions real or imagined, but that was a figurative expression. This was literal.

As a means of intimidation this would have been difficult to top, but it was precisely the type of behavior Mo feared might happen when natural enemies tried to work together. Officially this was termed a "food chain incident"—and Mo had taken steps to prevent these incidents. The business would have absolutely no chance of success if every time managers got angry, they ate their employees. This was considerably worse than a poor quarterly review. The cat was severely reprimanded and sent to an Appetite and Anger Management seminar. An incident report was made part of his permanent folder. He was removed from the management trainee program and transferred to a position in barn security.

Basically, Mo had to build the management infrastructure from dirt. Farmer Goode had run the farm just as his family had done it for decades. He purchased new machinery and upgraded equipment when it was necessary, but he had no interest in applying modern management techniques to the farm. He got up in the morning and milked the cows, collected the eggs, tilled the fields, and made repairs as necessary. When it was time, he harvested the crops and sheared the sheep. He was so busy every day just taking care of everyday chores that he didn't have time to worry about the next day.

Mo intended to run AAA Industries, Inc., as a state-of-the-industry agribusiness. As part of that program every job was analyzed to determine precisely what skills workers needed to do it well. Every job, from bottom to top, from the ants who seeded the fields to the birds in security assigned to see the fields. What strengths, abilities, and talents made it easier to do the job very well? What weaknesses made it more difficult? As Lionel had proven, weaknesses didn't make it impossible to do a certain job, but those weaknesses had to be recognized and allowances made for them.

Whenever possible, assistance was provided to help workers overcome obvious weaknesses. For example, Rocky "Red" Rooster's job in Corporate Communications required a voice loud enough to be heard. Unfortunately, as he added sponsors, his morning announcements grew considerably longer. So on occasion, Red got a sore gullet that made it very difficult for him to project his voice. To insure that he would be heard throughout the farm, and that those who held this job in the future could do the job, he was given a megaphone and plans were made to install an interfarm speaker system.

Those workers doing a good job in their current positions were rewarded. In recognition of the outstanding work Scarecrow was doing, he was promoted to a supervisory security position and given responsibility for guarding three fields from the crows. To assist him in this effort the farm purchased several thousand worms, which were trained to respond to any disturbance. These worms were distributed throughout the three fields, thus forming one of the most efficient early worming systems in the country.

Scarecrow was really excited about his promotion. It was the first time his hard work had been publicly recognized. "That's pretty good," Chucky said when Scarecrow told him about it. "I got to admit you've earned it." And then he added, "But you know you couldn't have done it without me."

Scarecrow looked at him as if he were crazy. "What are you talking about? I did it all myself. Take a look around. You see anybody else standing in the middle of this field keeping you away from the crops?"

Chucky cackled. "Nah, that's not what I mean. Lemme throw a little education your way. See, it's like this, without me being here every day—all right, every nice day—if I wasn't here to keep you on your pole, nobody would know if you were doing a good job or a bad job. You'd just be out here. You want to know the secret of success in business? It's simple. Satisfy the animals who depend on you. Your clients, customers, the turkey in the Shipping Department, the donkey who works next to you, the chickens who complain all the time—you give them what they need and they'll love you for it."

Scarecrow considered that. It did make sense. "So how did you help me?"

Chucky sighed. "Hey, pal, whattya got between those fake ears?"

"Nothing, remember?" Scarecrow had to admit sadly. "They forgot to give me a brain."

"Oh. Oh yeah. Well, see, I'm the constant threat that you protect the whole farm against. Maybe most of the animals don't give you enough credit because what you do isn't very exciting . . ." He paused. "Okay, I admit it, it's pretty boring, but if me and some of my pals get the seed, there's not going to be any wheat. If there's no wheat there's no harvest. No harvest, no money to keep this place going and no feed for anybody. So whether you like it or not, you need me. You and me, we're a team. So I'm pretty proud of our promotion."

Scarecrow had never thought about it that way before. He had never realized how important his one little job was to the prosperity of the entire farm. It was pretty impressive. "Okay," he admitted, "we're a team." After a pause he added, "But I get to be captain."

"Fine, fine, fine. But lemme ask you this. This promotion, does it mean maybe, you know, you're not going to be standing around here as much anymore?" Chucky asked hopefully.

SEVEN

Rules three and four appeared on the side of the barn the same day. Number three read, "A company is as strong as its weakest ant." And number four read, "Satisfy the donkey who worsk next to you."

Beau admitted that he didn't really understand that fourth rule, but Henrietta pointed out to him that "worsk" was spelled incorrectly and would be corrected. "It's supposed to be w-o-r-k-s," she explained. "Oh, I know that," he said. "What I mean is that I don't work next to a donkey."

With the exception of the occasional TV cameraman who roosted in a tree and filmed the farm at work, hoping to sell the footage to some independent station, media interest in the farm had faded. But the interest in the farm from businesspersons, animal rights groups, dependent farm animals, and Ed Biggs remained intense. Whatever the outcome of this extraordinary experiment, many, many lives would be changed, so both animals and nonanimals waited expectantly to see whether it would work.

At the end of its first year AAA Industries, Inc., showed a modest loss—not enough to threaten its immediate existence, but enough to make everyone nervous. The losses certainly could not continue.

Mo was confident that the structure was finally in place to insure the farm would succeed. He ran the business by the books, as many books as possible. He conducted the surveys, compiled the competencies, examined the 360s, and set up training classes. He posted the positive-thinking posters, tried to improve morale, and encouraged everyone to moo or baa or neigh up if they had something worth saying. So it was only a matter of time before he began to see results—that had to be true, it said so in all those books.

But in the meantime, they had to make immediate changes. Lawrence the Owl, having recently completed enough courses to earn a late-night television master's degree in economics, urged Mo to take the company public as a means to provide the needed investment capital.

Reluctantly, Mo agreed. Many of the animals were upset when they learned the farm stock was going to be offered to the public because this lowered the value of their founders' shares. They had no problem finding an underwriter, whom Abe—believing this was a terrible idea—insisted on referring to as "the undertaker." As the child labor case was still winding its way through the bureaucracy, the value of the stock was somewhat depressed, but the Initial Public Offering sold out within the first hour, and traded up throughout the day. Triple A closed at almost nine dollars, making many of the animals on the farm rich. At least on paper.

Over the water trough in the morning the only thing anyone wanted to talk about was what they were going to do with their money. They were prohibited from selling more than a few shares for eighteen months, but after that, as Queenie pointed out, it was definitely a Beau market.

The problem was that there was really very little that money could do for most of them. Food and shelter were already provided, although there was some discussion about catering. Georgina said she wanted to buy a car with bucket seats—so she could give her milk while driving to the beach. Joan had a much bigger dream: She wanted to produce a movie in which a courageous cow performs a heroic act to save the world from destruction. One of the ducks hinted darkly about buying a shotgun but refused to discuss his intentions. Lizzie intended to invest in technology and Cindy wanted to have cosmetic surgery—specifically, she wanted to have a beak job and get her wattle lifted. Piggy Banks was going to make his own CD, tentatively titled *This Little Piggy Goes to Town—in a Stretch Limo.* Scarecrow knew exactly what he would do with his money—he was going to buy a brand-new used suit!

Major agricompanies bought much of the stock, but a significant amount was purchased by "person or persons unknown"! Ed Biggs mortgaged several properties and used the cash to buy a substantial stake in Triple A. He couldn't lose. If the farm failed, the stock price would fall and he could buy a majority stake; if it succeeded, well, at least he'd make a profit.

The success of the offering relieved any immediate financial pressure on the farm and allowed Mo to focus on daily operations. Which was why one Thursday morning Scarecrow found himself sitting somewhat uneasily in Mo's office. "Congratulations," Mo told him, "you've done such a wonderful job guarding our fields that you've earned the opportunity to do something completely different."

Scarecrow could hardly believe his newly reglued ears. He was so good at his job that he didn't have to do it anymore! He was being promoted to an entirely different field where he would face new and exciting challenges. He felt strange; this must be what happy feels like, he decided. Mo explained that, based on the results of the tests and his success in the training courses, he was going to get his wish—he was going to be working in production. Specifically, he was assigned to the Female Chickens' Residence, which was being renamed Egg House.

Scarecrow was overwhelmed, but curious. "Who's

going to take over my old job? Who's going to guard the fields?"

"Don't worry about that," Mo replied. "We've got the perfect replacement for you. A Mr. Charles T. Crow has asked for the job . . ."

"What?" Scarecrow couldn't believe it. "He can't . . ."

Mo nodded firmly. "Yes, he can. He knows the fields almost as well as you do. He has plenty of experience. And he really wanted the job."

"Well, of course he wanted it," Scarecrow protested, but Mo had made his decision. Scarecrow started to argue, but stopped. It wasn't his concern.

Three days later, minutes after Rocky "Red" Rooster had finished his morning broadcast, Scarecrow reported for his first day of work in the exciting world of Egg Production. He was very nervous. And, truthfully, the girls in Egg Production were almost as nervous as he was. Being substantially bigger than anyone else, he was assigned a vacant nest on the lowest shelf. The girls watched carefully as he gently squatted into the position. Unfortunately, lacking knees, his legs shot straight out.

Clara looked at Henrietta and nodded appreciatively. The newcomer definitely had an interesting technique. As all egg layers know from experience, the key to performance is patience. One thing Scarecrow had proven through the years was that he definitely had patience.

For quite a long time, no one made the slightest cluck. Scarecrow could feel everybody staring at him, but he just looked straight ahead and waited, regularly squeezing his abdominal muscles as tightly as he could, just as he had been taught in training class. But nothing happened. Scarecrow had completed all his training courses, he had even scored well in such difficult courses as The Theory of Egg Laying, but he had never actually laid an egg.

This was the day he had been training for. E-Day. And as the minutes went by and he felt nothing happening he began to get even more nervous. He continued squeezing.

The girls didn't know what to say to him, although Cindy could barely take her eyes off him. Finally Lizzie asked sympathetically, "Is there anything you need? Maybe you'd like a comfortable pillow?"

He was embarrassed. He knew exactly what she meant: a training pillow. He shook his head. "No thank you," he said, and then could not think of anything else to say. Not one single word came into his head. He'd spent years standing in the field wishing he had someone, anyone, to talk to, he'd spent days and weeks and months preparing to talk to someone. Now, here he was with a coop full of hens and he had nothing to say to them. Desperate to start a conversation, he said politely to Clara, "Nice weather we're having today, isn't it?"

"Actually those are neon lights," she explained. "We have artificial lighting in here."

Scarecrow was so mortified he didn't say another word for several hours. He just sat there huffing and puffing and pushing and squeezing, doing everything he had been taught to do to produce an egg. Just one egg, he pleaded silently, please let me produce just one little egg.

His presence made everyone uneasy. Normally the coop would have been resounding with chatter, but there was none of the usual office banter, none of the friendly insults and challenges usually heard at work. Nobody told any jokes or loudly whispered the latest gossip. Instead, the girls who spoke did so in soft tones and their conversation was limited to the chicken sitting next to them.

Finally, after a couple of hours, the daily production began. "Incoming," a hen named Bertha on the third tier suddenly announced. Seconds later she produced the first egg of the day. Within minutes Joanna, sitting two tiers higher, shouted, "Big one coming!" and laid a beautiful egg. "Heeerrrreeeeeeee's money!" Hattie shouted as she dropped her quota. The department was swinging into full production. Scarecrow's presence was all but forgotten, as the glorious shouts started coming just about every minute. With whoops and cheers the girls egged each other on. "Call me Mama!" "Egg drop whoop!" "C'mon baby, c'mon, c'mon, c'mon, yeah! Home run!" As Lizzie laid her egg she yelled excitedly, "Cluck my name! Cluck my name!"

It was the worst day of Scarecrow's life. He tried everything he'd learned. He concentrated, he squeezed, he raised himself a few inches off his nest, his posture was textbook perfect—but he was not able to lay even a small egg. By the end of the day he was completely exhausted. "It's okay," Lizzie said calmly, taking him aside. "Believe me, everyone in this department has had days like this. It's just your first day, I know how much pressure there was on you, don't worry about it, you'll lay one down tomorrow. Remember," she added, quoting some business philosopher, "it isn't failure that matters, it's how you deal with failure."

Badly, was the answer to that question for Scarecrow, very badly. He felt like a complete failure. His hard-earned pride, his self-esteem, was gone. Scarecrow walked home alone that night, completely dejected.

In his old fields, though, there were quite a few happy birds. Chucky had determined to do a good job as Scarecrow's replacement. But he had spent so much time on the other side of the fence that it was difficult for him to make the adjustment. He was suddenly charged with guarding the same seeds he had lusted after for so long. And when his friends dropped in for a quick bite he had a difficult time turning them away.

For the first few hours, Chucky sat firmly on top of the pole, scanning the skies, and his will held solid. Finally, though, he decided that no one would miss one seed, one tiny little seed. So when no one was watching the watchbird, he hopped down from his perch and ate one seed. One delicious seed. That's all, he told himself, just one. But it was like eating the first chocolate-chip cookie in a brand-new box. Just one more, he decided, then I'm done. And he ate that second seed.

He was not the only one who struggled through the

day. Mo decided that Lily, with her sweet disposition and refined manners, would make a fine salesanimal. At his request she had completed the sales training courses and had been assigned to the Phone Sales Department. Mo's wife, Princess, the manager of that department, sat right next to Lily as she made her first actual sales call to produce wholesalers. "Hello, Mr. Stevens," she began, "would you like to buy some milk?"

"No," Stevens said gruffly. "Leave me alone."

"Thank you very much," Lily replied pleasantly. "It was very nice talking to you." Turning to Princess, she said, "Oh, this is fun."

Princess just stared at her. "Kid," she said, "I don't think you really get this game. Here, listen." Princess dialed and waited until the phone was answered. A man identified himself as Bill Garvey. "Bill, hey," she began, "it's Princess, over at Triple A. Maybe you've been reading about us in all the papers or seen some of the stories on television?"

Garvey admitted he'd heard something about it.

"Well, you know, we're sort of the hot ticket in town these days. People seem to love our milk. I thought maybe you'd be interested in discussing some sort of arrangement."

"I don't think so, Princess," he said. "I've got all the suppliers I need right now."

"I'm sure you do," Princess said. "I'll tell you what, though, I wish I had a dozen customers just like you."

There was a slight pause, then Garvey asked with

curiosity, "Whattya mean? I just told you I'm not interested in doing business with you. Why would you want a dozen customers like me?"

" 'Cause right now I've got about four dozen of 'em," she said with a sigh. Garvey laughed, and as soon as he stopped laughing Princess added, "Seriously Bill, you know there're a lot of people out there who are curious about us. You know, the whole animal farmer thing. If they knew you were carrying one of our products— maybe the sour cream or the buttermilk—there's a pretty good chance they'd want to give it a try. You might even pick up a couple of new accounts. And our prices are great. Guaranteed."

There was a slight pause. Princess winked at Lily. "All right," Garvey said, "I'll give it a shot."

Throughout the day Lily tried and tried. "You should buy our milk," she told one potential customer. "It comes directly from animals." After another potential customer turned her down and told her never to call him again, she said that she wished she had a dozen customers just like him. He replied, "Well that's just about the most ridiculous thing I've ever heard," and hung up.

The problem was that Lily was too sheepish, which is the primary occupational hazard faced by most sheep. If she had started the job with any confidence it quickly would have disappeared. But since she had absolutely no confidence in her ability to sell she had none to lose. As the days passed it became increasingly difficult for her to pick up the phone to face more rejection. "I can't make calls today," she would tell Princess. "I slipped and broke my voice last night." Or, "I can't dial any calls today, I cracked a hoof." Or, "I can't come to work today. I'm having a bad hair day over my entire body."

The Sales Womanager, as Princess insisted she be titled, was sympathetic. She had seen others struggle doing a job that did not come naturally to them. "You can do this," she told Lily, "I know you can. I'll help you." So Princess sat right next to Lily throughout much of that day and the days that followed, reviewing each phone call she made, making many suggestions, leaving only for brief periods to work with other members of her sales staff who asked for her assistance.

"Maybe you should give some of the others a little more help," Lily suggested.

"Nah," Princess explained, pointing her stubby tail toward the others, "those guys have a lot of experience. They could sell soft-boiled eggs to a hard-hearted chicken. They don't need my help as much as you do." Princess continued to work with Lily, even writing down the important sales points Lily might make. For example, she urged Lily to emphasize the fact that every product they sold was delivered fresh from the farm.

Grateful for the support, Lily returned to work determined to succeed. "Hello," she said to the next potential customer, "this is Lily from Triple A Industries, and I'd like to talk fresh with you . . ."

Jesse was also struggling. Not with his actual

work—no one on the farm worked harder than Jesse—
but with the paperwork. Or more accurately, the computer work. Three literate pigs and a field mouse
transferred to technology had written a software program that allowed the state of the farm to be updated
on a daily basis. Using this program it was possible to
find out exactly what work had been done anywhere on
the farm. If Mo needed to know how much manure had
been spread on the west field on Tuesday all he had to
do was check it on the computer. If he needed to chart
egg production over a week or a month or compare it
to another period he could do it. It was an important
tool. But keeping the program current meant that all
the managers and some members of the labor force had
to input data on a daily basis. Much of the work Jesse
did fell into no specific category; one day he might
clear a fallen tree from a field, the next day he would
pull the end of a rope to lift buckets from a well. It was
his responsibility to note this on the computer.

Unfortunately, computer keyboards were not designed for size-twenty-three hooves. It often took Jesse
hours to record the work he had done. And because of
his limited typing skills, he often got it wrong. So
"clearing the well" became "cleaning the bell." "Carrying a load" became "marrying a toad," which immediately became a popular joke on the farm: "Jesse's out
marrying another toad." And because Queenie wanted
him stabled at a reasonable hour so they could put on
the feed-bag together, he began coming in from the

field earlier and earlier to record his workday on the computer.

Queenie recognized that Jesse needed help with his computer skills. Being a good manager, Queenie helped him overcome this weakness by enrolling him in two computer training classes and having a little clip soldered to the side of his hoof that would hold a stick. He could use the stick to hit the proper keys. He began practicing for hours and hours.

Rapidly now, the company began to falter. After almost a full month working in Production, Scarecrow had yet to lay his first egg. After the first few awkward days the girls accepted his presence; they had even begun giving him inside tips, but nothing helped. For a while everyone assumed it was just anxiety. But after the first few eggless weeks some animals began wondering if he really had it in him. For the first time Scarecrow felt the unpleasant emotion known as shame. He continued to sit there, hour after hour, day after day, staring straight ahead, wondering if all his training had been a complete waste of time.

Chucky was doing even worse. Left alone to guard fields of seed, he was powerless against temptation. He had gained almost a pound. He could barely lift off the ground to his perch. So far he had successfully managed to cover his claw prints, but he knew his deception would be discovered when whole portions of the field failed to sprout. That would mark the end of his career as a workingbird, he knew, and when he thought about that he too felt a new emotion: sadness.

Since the first day the phone bank was installed, Oliver, an eastern screech owl with a naturally booming voice and the personality to match it, had been one of Princess's best salesanimals. Occasionally, though, even Oliver had a bad streak and needed some friendly reassurance. In the past, Princess had always been right there to supply it. "You de bird!" she'd tell him. Or, "A hoot and a holla and you've made another dolla." And when things got real tough, as they sometimes have for every salesbeing since the beginning of selling, she'd take him out for some flies just to relax.

But since Lily joined the sales staff she had been the focus of Princess's attention. "Princess's project," they all called Lily. Princess no longer seemed to have time to spend a few minutes with the other members of her staff. She was also getting a little lax in her paperwork. The staff didn't seem to be receiving as many cold leads as before. And they were definitely not getting the normal amount of sales-support information—articles from newspapers and magazines, such as, "Studies show whole milk prevents hair loss in lab mice," that she had always seemed to find. She even pretty much stopped hanging her motivational messages—"*No* is only a speed bump on the road to *Yes!*" "Milk! Every call you make!" "The Sellers' Bible: Thou shalt bill!"—that they all laughed about, but in fact loved.

When Oliver finally discussed the situation with Princess, she got very defensive. "Suppose one day in the darkest woods you found a young bird that didn't know how to fly alone," she said. "So you took her home and worked with her every day until she could soar on her own. Would it be fair to keep her at home or would you let her fly as high and far as her wings would take her?"

The point she was making, Oliver understood, was that she had worked with each member of the sales staff until he or she was able to prosper without her help. She didn't think he needed her help anymore, but she knew that Lily did. "I see what you mean," he told her excitedly, "and something just like that really happened to me. I found a baby robin that had fallen out of its nest. I brought her home and fed her. As she grew up I took her outside to learn how to fly and finally one day she could fly on her own. I took her to a field, gave her a little peck, and let her go."

"You do understand," Princess said.

"Not exactly," Oliver concluded. "She flew straight right into a wall. Bam! Straight into it. Broke a wing. And you know what I learned from that? Just because you're a bird doesn't mean you're going to be a good flyer. Or even a good singer. Some birds just aren't very good at flying. Trust me, I've heard birds who sing off-key."

Princess thought about that, but she found it a little confusing. Was he trying to tell her that she would never be able to teach a sheep to fly?

Meanwhile, Jesse actually did get a little bit better on the computer. The training classes took up a lot of his time, but he gained important skills. The stick made it possible for him to hit the right key more often. He spent so many hours each night practicing that he was often exhausted in the morning and kind of ran out of energy in the afternoon, but he successfully cut down the time it took him to record his daily efforts. Of course, part of the reason for that was that the time he had to spend in the field actually working declined dramatically, so he had much less to record. Queenie was so proud of his hard work that to celebrate his accomplishment she bought him a wonderful present: Microsoft's brand-new program Office for Thoroughbreds.

Problems similar to these had arisen in just about every department as the animals struggled to master new competencies and fit comfortably into their new jobs. Several animals had been placed in positions for which they lacked the knowledge, skills, or—most important—talent. No matter what all the surveys and tests reported, no matter how long they had been on the farm or how well-liked they were, they just weren't qualified. As a result the farm was no longer functioning smoothly.

For quite some time the price of the stock remained stable and relatively high. But Mo knew that if the news leaked out that a scarecrow was working in Egg Production, a crow was guarding the seeds, a workhorse was struggling to master a computer, and all the other problems they were having, the effect could be disastrous. When he looked out at the beautiful fields he could almost see a fast-food restaurant there—and shuddered at the thought it would be serving baconburgers!

Mo had managed to keep the internal problems private. So it was a great surprise to everyone when the *Daily Times* ran a long story about the farm, a story that reported: "An unnamed source claimed that the farm was encountering significant problems in many departments, among them falling egg production and sparsely seeded fields. Revenues are falling from last quarter's high as the sales force struggles . . ."

No one could imagine how the newspaper obtained this information. "I just don't understand how they could have found out about all of this," Mo said to Lawrence.

Lawrence was furious. "Well," he responded angrily, "I'd sure like to find the stool pigeon who told them all this. I can't imagine who it was."

But the damage was done. The next morning everybody was hard at work when the quiet was shattered by Clara running frantically through the barnyard squawking madly, "The stock is falling! The stock is falling!"

EIGHT

By the time rule number five, "Everyone should be well rounded," appeared on the side of the barn the other rules, painted only months earlier, were already chipping and fading. And that was certainly symbolic of the state of the once-beautiful farm. Clara had been absolutely right—the stock price had fallen drastically. That, combined with the operating losses, put the continued existence of AAA Industries, Inc., in jeopardy. And the chilling fact was that for the animals on the farm that also threatened their continued existence as live stock.

The only animal on the entire farm who derived even the slightest benefit from the situation was Ringolette, whose anxiety—combined with the morning jogs the cows were taking to increase stamina—

had caused her to lose fifty-five pounds. In fact, she was less rounded than she had ever been.

"She still looks beautiful," Farmer Goode said, rocking gently on the front porch of his old house. On a lovely Sunday afternoon he'd returned to the farm for the very first time to see all his old friends.

"Well, she's lost more than fifty pounds," Mo replied, "but still . . . she's a big cow."

Farmer Goode seemed confused. "Oh, Ringolette? No, I meant the whole place. Looks like you're doing a good job, Mo. I knew you would."

"I wish," he said almost to himself, "I wish. Farmer Goode," he finally admitted, "I have to be honest with you. We're in trouble. I've read every business book I could find. I've been trying to use all the best management methods, but . . . but it isn't working." A single tear formed in the corner of his eye and rolled gently down his long, long snout.

Just then Piggy Banks jogged by screaming loudly, "Moink, moink."

Farmer Goode watched him in amazement. "What the tarnation was that?" He turned to Mo. "Wasn't that the Aristotle kid? What kind of noise was that he was making?"

"He's doing some training," Mo admitted somewhat reluctantly. "He's practicing cow herding. Unfortunately, he's having some problems learning a second language. See, we want all the animals on the farm to be well-rounded, to be good at a lot of different things."

"Yes sir, I see," Farmer Goode agreed, "I definitely

see." After a moment of silence, he leaned back in his rocker, took a long silent drag on his pipe, and told Mo the secret of his success. "Let me tell you a little story, Mo. You know, when I took over the farm from my father I wanted to bring in all the new ways. I read all the books. I consulted the experts." He laughed at a distant memory. "One time, I remember, when transcendental meditation was the biggest thing, I brought one of them gurus to teach all the animals how to meditate. I figured if they were calm they'd work better. This fella did all his ooming and ahhhming and the next thing I knew all the animals were in some kind of deep trance. One of them, in fact, was your great-great-grandfather."

"Really?" Mo was amazed. "What happened?"

"Took us three days to get everybody back to normal. And a couple of goats walked off the farm saying they were going to live on a mountain in Tibet. We never heard a baa from them again.

"The point is, Mo, I tried everything. And then one day I realized that the best thing I could be was me. I was a farmer. I know, you look at me and you think movie hunk, astronaut, private detective, a minister, but the fact is that I was a farmer, from the gunk on my boots to the hair-growing slop I put on my head. I was a farmer and I was good at it and it was what I loved doing most.

"After a while I left the animals alone, and they pretty much figured out the same thing I did. So from then on I made sure every animal was doing what he or she was best at doing. I gave them as much support as I could, plenty of good nutritious food . . ." He paused here, and sighed. ". . . 'cept maybe for that health food thing I tried in the eighties . . . good shelter, all the tools they needed and a big dose of encouragement. I kept it simple: What's your work, who you are, how you gonna get there. Sure, we had our problems, every business does from time to time, but overall, it worked out fine."

Mo glanced at the growing pile of management books that was threatening to collapse the porch. "But what about all those books?"

"Oh," Farmer Goode said, "those books are very important. In fact, there's a few of them that are real good. I found the best ones pretty much relied on common sense—the sort of things that I already knew but I didn't know that I knew, if you know what I mean.

"The rest of them—particularly those big thick ones with all the highfalutin' theories, they're real important too. You best keep 'em somewhere real safe and dry, because if one night in December, God forbid, you should happen to run out of firewood those books'll work just fine."

Mo laughed. Having read all those books he thought he had learned about every possible mannagement technique. But here was a new one for him: common sense. It might work, he thought, it could work, it was possible. "Wait. What about all the surveys and forms and interviews and 360s and . . ."

Farmer Goode put up a hand to stop him. "Well,

you bet they're real important," he explained. "It can get dang cold in January too."

Later that night Mo watched the taillights of Farmer's Goode's car fade into the distance. And he felt renewed. He had a whole new plan: There would be no more new plans!

He knew it would take time to make this new business plan work, and it was questionable that he had that time. Somehow the newspapers continued to find out about every problem on the farm, large or small, and they ran several stories predicting the demise of the company. "The interesting animalogical experiment seems to have failed," wrote one, "as the animals, it appears, turned out to be animals." As a result the stock continued to fall and potential investors were scared away.

Biggs sat in his office reading yet another such story. "Fine job, Homey," he said to the pigeon, "perhaps you'd like some more corn?" Biggs's tiny heart was overflowing with joy. His plan was perfect. When the price of the stock hit bottom he would scoop up a majority of the shares and close down that infernal farm. It would not be long, he was certain, until he would be having that pig Mo for breakfast. With eggs!

To Mo's great surprise, even he did not know about all of the problems cited in the article. The situation was even worse than he feared: "Sparsely seeded fields," he wondered, how could that be? The ants in distribution had done a wonderful job. But to be certain he trotted out to the fields to inspect them for himself.

He was met in the field by an unusually plump crow. "This new job," Chucky said as he tried to explain his seed belly. "You know how it is, boss. I've had to do a lot of sitting around."

But when Mo looked around he was stunned. "The seed," he said, "where is it? What happened to it?"

"Oh yeah," Chucky said. "That's another thing I've been meaning to talk to you about. You've heard how popular seedless watermelon is, right?" Mo admitted he had heard that. "Well, I figured we could do better than that. We're going to produce seedless seed!" Even Chucky was impressed with that one.

Mo immediately took action to save the harvest. "Mistakes are made," Mo told Chucky. "Sometimes the crow gets hired to guard the seed."

"Definitely a mistake," Chucky agreed.

Mo tried to figure out the most logical thing to do. It turned out to be pretty simple. "And when they happen the only thing to do is correct them as quickly as possible. When you recognize a problem, you can't just ignore it. I'm afraid we're going to have to let you fly."

Chucky knew it was inevitable. "But where am I gonna go?" he asked.

"I'm sorry, but there's nothing I can do about it," Mo said honestly. Then he watched sadly as Chucky hopped once, twice, and on his third effort barely managed to get into the air, flapping his wings rapidly as he tried to retain his dignity, and flew away.

Mo had to admit that this particular effort was a failure. Promoting Scarecrow to a job for which he obviously had no natural talent had been a terrible mistake. Scarecrow hadn't laid a single egg and his replacement in Security had eaten the seeds he was supposed to be guarding. In an effort to reward Scarecrow, who had been exceptional in his original field, two positions had been weakened.

Although it was hard for Scarecrow to admit it, he accepted the fact that he wasn't right for his new job. His self-esteem had disappeared long ago. He was lost, and trapped. So he was actually relieved when Mo came to Egg House and spoke with him. "You were the best there ever was at your old job," Mo said. "And the best you can ever be in Production is mediocre. It just isn't the right job for you. Look, we need you to go back to your old field."

Scarecrow knew this to be true, but still, he was embarrassed. Instead of the respect that he had so desperately craved, he had been publicly humiliated. He had to go back to a much less prestigious job. Scarecrow sighed, and nodded. He couldn't speak.

Mo understood, and tried to lessen the impact. "The truth is that we really need you in the fields. So here's what we're going to do. I'm promoting you to Head of Field Security for the entire farm. That's an extremely important job. We're going to make you Vice-President of Security and pay you more than you were earning in Production."

Scarecrow could not believe it. Vice-President? Him? A scarecrow? In the entire history of scarecrowdom, no scarecrow had ever been promoted to Vice-

President. And better pay too? Everybody knew that field work didn't pay as well as production. "How . . . how can you do that?" he asked Mo.

"It's simple. Just look around at these ladies. They're different from you." He paused, then added firmly, "Real different. Most of them like doing what they do, and they do it very well. Just like you do such a good job in Security. Let's be realistic, that's the job you were made to perform. So congratulations, Mister Head of Field Security."

The girls in Egg Production were sorry to see him go, but proud of him in his new ragged suit, torn hat, and carefully scuffed shoes. "You're so lucky," Cindy said somewhat enviously.

"Really?" Scarecrow said, quite surprised. No one had ever called him that before. "Lucky? Me?"

"Absolutely. You're your own boss, you make your own hours, you get to work outside . . . Look at us, we have to lay around here all day." She hesitated and looked up sweetly at him. "Um, maybe I could come to your field to visit you one day."

Scarecrow knew that if he were a robot instead of a strawman his bolts would be popping. So much had happened so quickly. The farm needed him. Needed him! And this cute chick wanted to visit him. "That would be very nice," he told her. "I think I'd like that." And when he walked away, it was with his head held high.

In the Sales Department Lily also realized that she had made a very bad mistake. She'd put a bright red polish on the nails of all four of her feet instead of her usual passion pink, making her look too much like a fire engine for her comfort. She had also accepted the fact that she was never going to be a good salesanimal. "It's true," she told Princess. "There are two kinds of animals in this world, salesanimals and buyers. And what I'm really good at is buying."

That realization came to her during a cold call to a local seamstress who perhaps needed some wool. "Oh, I'd love to buy your wool," the woman said, "but unfortunately I still have all these absolutely adorable woolen sweaters left over from last season . . ."

"Really?" Lily replied, her ears perking up. "What color adorable sweaters?" It turned out to be a disastrous sales call for Lily. She spent two weeks' salary on sweaters.

Of course Lily wasn't the only member of the Sales Department not doing well. Sales of eggs, milk and milk products, the crops, and every product were way down. At a meeting with Oliver, once the most productive member of her sales staff, Princess asked, "What's wrong? What are we doing differently? What's going on?"

"I know you, right?" he replied. "I'd recognize that pigtail anywhere. You're, um . . . you're . . . Sandra Bullock—no, that's not it. I know, Sheryl Crow. No, no that's not it. Miss Piggy, is that you?"

Princess got the message. "Okay, I get it. I know I haven't been spending as much time with everybody as

I used to, but I didn't think you needed my help any-more."

"Pull up some mud, Princess," he suggested. "Let me explain something to you. You ever watch a flock of birds in flight?" Many times, she responded. Oliver continued, "The first thing they taught us in flight school was that the most wind resistance is at the point of the traditional V-formation, so the strongest bird should always fly point. But after a while even the strongest bird flying point is going to get tired. So it drops back into the flock and another bird takes the lead. The real point is that no matter how strong any one bird is, it can't do it alone. It needs help."

"But I was trying to help someone who really needed my help," Princess protested. "I was just trying to be a good manager."

"Well, you managed to alienate most of your sales staff. Look, we all like Lily, but by spending so much time helping her you couldn't give us the time we needed. So everybody suffered. There's a reason birds don't fly an X-formation. That would force just about every bird to fight the wind. And the result of you try-ing to be a good manager was that Lily didn't get much better and everybody else got worse."

Princess was devastated. "Maybe I should have been spending more time with my best animals, huh? The ones who make the difference? I guess I screwed up big time, didn't I?"

"Don't be so hard on yourself. The second thing they taught us in flight school was that when you crash into a wall, you shake it off and get back up in the air before the cat gets you."

In the stable Jesse was exhausted. After a hard day's work in the field, he was standing over the computer painfully typing one letter at a time. Queenie walked over and stood next to him, lovingly flipping her tail over his haunches. Moving closer to her, he forced a smile. "This is just really hard for me," he said, nodding at the monitor, his frustration just shy of real anger. "I don't understand this thing at all. Look, it's telling me to take a megabyte of ram. Why would I want to do that? Every ram I've ever known has been a pretty decent guy. Why would I want to bite one of them?"

"Here," she said, giving him several lumps of sugar, "this'll calm you down." Queenie had reached the inescapable conclusion that on a computer Jesse would never be more than barely adequate. "You know what," she said, "I have a great idea. From now on you take care of the horsework and I'll enter your data into the computer."

He neighed. "Thank you, sweetheart, but it's my data. I've gotta do it."

She whipped her tail from side to side. "Now that is absolutely ridiculous. What a big strong guy like you should be doing is focusing on what you do well. That's good for the entire farm. Let's face it, Jess, you're never going to be very fast on the computer. So why waste your time struggling with it when somebody else can do it for you, freeing you to do what you do better than anybody else on the whole farm." She looked at him sternly. "And that is right from this horse's mouth!"

Mo's management policies had created serious problems in just about every department. For example, Abe the Goat, who was running the Customer Complaint Department, had developed his own unique style of dealing with callers. Usually, a caller would begin the conversation by saying something as simple as, "I've got a problem."

"You bet you do," Abe would respond aggressively. "You got me on the other end of the phone. I hope you're not thinking maybe that's a good thing?"

"No, no," the caller would inevitably explain, "I mean, I've got a complaint."

"C'mon, what do you have to complain about? You want something to complain about, you should have my knees. It's amazing I can still walk without falling down and breaking something. Talk about breaking things, let me tell you about my aunt Rosey . . ."

"Maybe you don't understand, I just want to make a little complaint. I mean, it's nothing—"

"A little complaint, huh? Sure. All day long, that's all I hear, whine, whine, whine. Listen to me, nobody likes a complainer. So just get over it. Instead of complaining . . ."

It was somewhat revealing that Mo received more complaints about the Complaint Department than any other department on the entire farm. As a result, Lily was moved into Customer Service, where her strongest talents, her pleasing personality and gracious manner, would prove the most valuable to the farm. Naturally, she was immediately successful.

Abe the Goat, meanwhile, was transferred into quality control, where he too was able to utilize his talents. "Sweetheart, you call this an egg? Look, Shelly, may I call you Shell? Good. So, listen to me, this is not an acceptable egg, Shell. Seems to me maybe you're standing up on the job."

Throughout the farm scenes like these were repeated over and over as managers and employees found more productive ways to accomplish their work. Mo held a series of meetings with his managers to explain his new policy: Normalcy. Rationality. Good sense.

Princess was very impressed, wondering, "When did they come up with those revolutionary ideas?"

Under this new policy, managers made a determined effort to discover each animal's strengths and insure that each one was doing a job that emphasized those strengths. Animals with obvious talents, like milk producers Joan, Paula, Georgina, and Ringolette, were made to feel secure and provided with whatever assistance they needed. To keep top performers like Scarecrow in important but less prestigious jobs, these workers were given substantially better benefits than workers doing jobs normally considered higher on the ladder to the top of the silo. When weaknesses affected job performance, like Jesse struggling with the computer, managers found methods to assist them. Managers were urged to meet often with each employee and focus on providing support for their most productive workers, rather than spending valuable time trying to bring less-talented workers up to an acceptable level. And if—like Chucky—workers failed at a job, or to use the old expression, if they laid an egg, they were set free or moved to a completely different job.

Gradually the changes began to take effect. Production began to increase. Once again, crops began to grow in the fields. Spirits and morale improved as most animals found themselves doing jobs they were good at and that they enjoyed—and for which their achievements were recognized and fairly rewarded. In turn, this made it much less desirable for them to continue to strive for promotion to a job on a higher level primarily for the prestige and benefits that it would bring.

Once the animals had been put in the right jobs, provided the tools they needed and given strong management support, spirit and morale kept improving. And as they did, Mo noted with satisfaction, so did production.

Unfortunately, though, negative stories about the farm continued to appear in the media. While some of the wilder stories were indeed based on real events—a mouse was driving a tractor, for instance, although he absolutely did not take it drag-racing downtown. And indeed, there was a pig who sang rap, but he definitely did not have a tattoo on his rump boasting *"It's a Pig Country!"* Other stories were entirely fictitious. For example, no chickens were accidentally fried by touching a downed power line. And the cows were not so bitter at events that they were producing sour cream. The sheep definitely had not resorted to Rogaine© baths to induce excessive hair growth. And Scarecrow had not had extensive cosmetic surgery that had completely ruined his ability to scare.

True or not, the stories were damaging to the corporation. The stock price remained low. But still, no one could figure out where the reporters were getting their information. That was exactly what Scarecrow was thinking about as he hung out one brilliant summer afternoon. Since returning to his fields as the new Vice-President of Security he had done a superb job. Very few seeds had been lost.

It had not been easy. Soon after Scarecrow had returned to his post Chucky showed up all alone. "It's you and me again, pal," Chucky crowed, "just like old times. You ready to rumble?"

Scarecrow could detect the phony bravado backing that challenge. "Hey, how you doing, Chucky?" he asked.

"Ah, you know me, 'Crow," Chucky admitted, "just floating on the winds of life."

"What happened to all your friends—the ones you let eat the seed?"

Chucky cawed. "It was pretty funny, soon's they found out I couldn't give 'em seed anymore, whzzzzzzzzzzzz . . . they flew off."

"How come you didn't go with them?"

Chucky shrugged his wings. "I don't know, really. I guess I sort of got to like it around here."

Scarecrow felt a smile on his face, even if he couldn't show it. "Well," he said firmly, "the rules haven't changed. I'm not letting you get any seed from these fields."

"Oh yeah?" Chucky said in a voice that contained the first hint of excitement. "You and what army?"

And so that particular battle was rejoined. As before, most often Scarecrow won, but the daily skirmishes were fought well. Chucky quickly lost most of the weight he'd gained and got back to his flying weight. And just as quickly Scarecrow's new clothes had gotten perfectly ripped and dirty, just the way Scarecrow liked them.

Although the threats of bankruptcy and prosecution for using child labor hung over the farm like a dark storm cloud, life had pretty much returned to normal. Rocky "Red" Rooster's morning announcements had gotten mercifully brief as most of his advertising disappeared. Mary was promoted to Chief Financial Officer, joining Mo's staff. And Miles asked for Lily's paw in breeding, an offer she happily accepted.

One August morning, Scarecrow was hard at work when suddenly a thought hit him. Or at least he believed it was a thought. It just as easily could have been a pebble; he just didn't have thoughts often enough to clearly identify the feeling when one of them hit him. Whatever it was, it drew his attention to the wide-open blue sky. He scanned the horizon and saw nothing—which really bothered him. He watched the sky for several minutes, and still saw nothing. It took him a long time to figure out why.

"Hey, Chucky," he yelled, "you see anything strange?"

Chucky searched the sky and the land. "I don't see nothing," he reported.

"Exactly," Scarecrow said. "Nothing's there. Doesn't that bother you?"

"Maybe you been standing out in the sun too long," Chucky suggested. "You want me to get you some water?"

Scarecrow told him what was bothering him. Since his promotion to Vice-President and Head of Field Security, there had never been a day—from dawn to dusk—when more than a few minutes had passed without his spotting at least one pigeon, one member of the Hawks gang, making wide sweeps across the farm. They were there all the time. They were there so often they seemed to have become a permanent part of the skyscape. He'd become accustomed to seeing them. And now they were gone. It was the absence of the pigeons that attracted his attention—and made him very, very nervous. "Listen, Chucky," Scarecrow yelled, "you looking for a job?"

Chucky perked up. "I . . ." he stammered, "I . . . you know what happened the last time I had a job?"

"Yeah, yeah, I know," Scarecrow replied. "So now we know what your main weakness is. We'll just make sure not to put you in a position where that weakness becomes important. Besides, I got a pretty good idea I know what your best talent is. The thing is, I need you."

After considering Scarecrow's offer for a fraction of a second, Chucky accepted with great enthusiasm. "Okay, boss," he said, "you got the Chuck bird. Exactly what do you want me to do?"

The Hawks returned the next morning, in force. Throughout the day six or seven pigeons flew above the farm, alighting frequently on a windowsill or a railing or even on the ground in the barnyard, staying there for a few minutes, then flying up to the telephone wire where their gang leader, Squash, and his right-claw bird, Homey, sat waiting.

This time, though, Scarecrow and Chucky the Crow watched them carefully.

About four o'clock in the afternoon Squash said something to Homey, and Homey took off, flying west, toward town. A minute later, after exchanging glances with Scarecrow, Chucky also took off, also flying west. He flew easily and gracefully, his strong wings catching the slightest breeze. If he had looked back he would have seen Scarecrow watching him closely, knowing he carried the fate of the company with him.

Two days later Ed Biggs was just sitting down to a big dinner in his big house when there came an unexpected knock at his door. To Biggs's surprise, Mo was standing there on all four legs. Lawrence was sitting on his back. "Ah, gentleanimals," Biggs said happily. He felt quite confident he knew the reason for their visit.

They had finally realized that it was futile to resist his offer any longer. "Come in, come in."

As they went past his dining room on the way to the parlor Mo saw Biggs's dinner waiting on a platter: A chicken had been roasted! A cold chill ran through his body from snout to tail. If Biggs noticed it he gave no indication. He was too busy savoring his victory. "I guess I can't offer you anything . . . to eat, can I?" And then he laughed.

When they finally sat down in the parlor, Biggs asked, "What can I do for you?"

"You can sell us all your stock," Mo responded, "for half the market price."

Lawrence added, "And go away and never bother us again."

Biggs was taken aback. "But . . . why would I do something that foolish?"

"We know what you've been doing, Biggs," Mo told him. "We know where the newspapers have been getting their information about the farm. And we know how you've been getting your information."

Biggs was shocked. "How . . . what . . ." He was completely flustered, but recovered quickly. "And . . . what difference does it make how I found out?" he sneered. "There's nothing you can do about it."

"Maybe," Mo agreed. "But it seems that you've been giving that information to the newspaper—you even made up some of the stories—and then you bought and sold stock based on the stories that you knew were going to be published."

"I think that's called . . . bad manners," Lawrence said, "and also insider trading. The difference between the two of them is you can't go to jail for bad manners." He shook a wing at him. "Not nice."

Biggs glared at Mo. "You pig," he spewed, "you can't prove a thing. You don't have any evidence."

This time Mo smiled. "Maybe you'd better check your computer—the 'farm stock' file? The one where you listed all your phone calls, who you spoke to, the amount of stock you traded . . ."

Biggs was rushing toward his computer even before Mo stopped speaking. "Nobody can get inside my computer," he said defiantly. As he sat down he reached for the mouse—and the mouse ran away. Biggs leaped back in surprise, and just barely saw Lionel Engine scoot to safety.

Biggs's anger was rising so rapidly he could barely contain it. He started shaking. He stood up, his chair fell backward, and with venom in his voice he warned Mo, "None of this matters. Do you hear me, none of it. I have friends in the government . . ." He leaned forward and said, "And they are going to put you out of business for using child labor." Then he started laughing. "Child labor, that's a good one." Finally he stopped. "And so, you big fat pig, what do you have to say to me now!" It was more of a threat than a question.

But Mo was not threatened. Time seemed frozen, Biggs hovering above Mo and Lawrence, waiting for an answer. Mo cleared his throat. "Mr. Biggs," he said pleasantly, "I just happened to notice when we came in that you were eating an innocent chicken for dinner."

"And?" Biggs responded. "Your point is . . ."

Suddenly, Mo stood up on his hind legs, towering over Biggs. Biggs stepped back. "Tell me, Biggs," Mo demanded firmly, "just how old do you think that chicken you were eating was? Because if the government decides that the child labor laws should be applied to animals on the farm, then you . . ."

"No," Biggs said, as the horrible truth swept over him, "no. You don't understand. It was a chicken, that's all, it doesn't matter how old it—you tricked me!" He screamed, "You tricked me! You tricked me!"

Mo and Lawrence left Biggs's house carrying his agreement to sell them all his stock for a price even lower than they were ready to pay. Biggs was curled up in an easy chair, his head buried between his knees, rocking back and forth.

As they walked out the door, Lawrence paused. "I have a suggestion for you, Mr. Biggs," he said. "Next time you'd be better off eating . . . pigeon!"

EPILOGUE

 From that day on all the animals on the farm lived relatively happily ever after. Life wasn't perfect—as everyone knows, it never is—but with Biggs removed forever as a threat they were able to move forward quite successfully.

Mo certainly didn't completely abandon the use of surveys to make the farm run more efficiently. When used properly they were extremely valuable tools. So he determined precisely what information management really could use and used brief, focused surveys to obtain it. That enabled him to measure basic farm values, such as job satisfaction and worker-management relationships. He even used a short survey to find out what the farm's customers liked and disliked—and gave them more of what they liked and corrected those things they didn't like.

Other tools, such as the competencies and 360s, continued to be used in a limited way—which meant they focused directly on those skills that could be learned, and where improvements needed to be made. But the real focus was on helping animals meet their goals and achieve desired outcomes.

For his role in uncovering Biggs's plot Scarecrow was asked to join the Executive Committee and became one of the most respected individuals in the company. Great praise was lavished on Chucky, who tried very hard to remain humble. "Ah, it was nothing," he said, "I was just doing my job."

Mo pointed out to him that just doing his job might have saved the whole farm. "It doesn't matter what job you do, whether it's big or small," he said at the awards ceremony, "whether it seems important or menial. As Mr. Charles T. Crow proved, anyone can make a difference. You can be a hero in any role."

The whole astonishing story was told by Piggy Banks in a song titled "Grilled Pigeon," which led to his signing a recording contract and the release of his breakthrough CD, *Songs for Vegetarians,* which went platinum and established him as America's most popular rapping pig.

Piggy Banks wasn't the only animal to leave the farm. After receiving a tremendous amount of publicity for successfully breaking into Biggs's computer, Lionel Engine finally realized that driving a tractor was not the thing he did best and gave it up—and then accepted an offer from NASCAR to drive in their circuit.

And at dawn each morning on the AAA Industries, Inc., farm Rocky "Red" Rooster woke everyone with his amplified calls, which included the schedule of coming events he'd added. Minutes later, Scarecrow would leave his home to stand guard another day over all his friends on the farm. But the last thing he did each morning as he departed was to lean over and give Cindy a peck on her beak.

Scarecrow had found happiness.

LEARN MORE

To find out about the management discoveries, research, and insights that inspired this story, please go to the Animals, Inc. Book Center at the *Gallup Management Journal* (http://gmj.gallup.com). Managers looking to maximize their companies' performance should visit www.gallup.com/management.

Animals, Inc. readers can receive a six-month trial subscription to the *Gallup Management Journal*. Simply go to http://commerce.gallup.com/ma/code/ and follow these instructions:

1. Enter the following promotional code and click "continue." Promotional Code: 11200214417810 6606.
2. Review your subscription information and click "continue" if it is correct.
3. If you already have a Gallup membership, enter your e-mail address and password, then click "continue." After you read and agree to the subscriber agreement, your subscription process is complete.

4. If you do not have a Gallup membership, you will need to create one. Enter your e-mail address. Select "No," then click "continue." Complete the member registration information, click "continue," and read and agree to the subscriber agreement.

For questions or assistance, go to: galluphelp@ gallup.com.

ACKNOWLEDGMENTS

This book is the brainchild of many talented and creative people, most especially the late Don Clifton, father of strengths psychology, great storyteller, mentor, and teacher, who taught us to soar with our strengths. As will millions of people around the world whose lives he touched and inspired, we will always remember Don for the way he used his strengths to help us get the most out of ours.

Thanks to Jim Clifton, Gallup's chairman and CEO, whose commitment to talent drives excellence throughout our organization. Jim always challenges us to be better than we ever thought we could be. And his storytelling instincts are superb.

To the Gallup authors Curt Coffman, Marcus Buckingham, Gabriel Gonzalez-Molina, Benson Smith, and Tony Rutigliano: Thank you for laying the clear path that this book follows. To the great seminar leaders and consultants BC Christenson, Barry Conchie, Maribel Cruz, Bernadine Karunaratne, Dan Kingkade, Curt Liesveld, Mary Pat Loos, Charles McClendon, Jacque Merritt, Jeannie Ruhlman, Robyn Seals, Tim Simon, and others, thank you, for it is in your labors that we see the message of this book lived.

To the wise women and men like Cheryl Beamer, Jan Miller, Jane Miller, Connie Rath, and Tom Rath. Your healthy mixture of love, candor, and tact always kept us steadfast in our mission.

To the people who direct our movement every working day, Sarah Van Allen, Caren Ashmon, Lynn Genovese, Amanda Hokanson, and Kianna Riley, thank you for making good things happen. To all those who took time out of their busy schedules to read and give very important and helpful feedback, Michael Allen, Steve Caines, Sean Dollie, Erin Doyle, Sue Lyle, Kusum Ram, Tom Rieger, and Kendra Tucker. To all of our associates at Gallup, thank you for the support and encouragement over the last three years. Your faith and confidence have brought us to this point.

Very special thanks to Larry Emond, whose brilliant ideas never cease; to Geoff Brewer, our Gallup editor and all-around great guy; and to Brian Brim, whose insights permeate this entire book.

We would also very much like to thank David Fisher, without whose creativity, wonderful sense of humor, and hard work this book would not have been possible.

Our thanks also go to our editors, Rick Wolff and Colin Fox, and to everyone else at Warner Books for their enthusiastic partnership, their exacting standards, and their superb ideas.

And the deepest of thanks to our spouses and best friends, Judy and Jeff, for all of their love and inspiration.